Microsoft® Office 98
Step by Step

Macintosh® Edition

Word Processing with Word

Presentations with PowerPoint

Spreadsheets with Excel

Computer
Literacy
Press

Cincinnati, Ohio

Bonita Sebastian

Design / InfoTech / Paul Quin
Cover / Carolyn Ayres
Production coordination / Zipporah Collins
Copyediting / Tad Lathrop
Technical checking / Tad Lathrop
Page layout / Computer Literacy Press, Inc.
Imagesetting / Data Reproductions Corporation
Printing and binding / Data Reproductions Corporation

Microsoft® is a registered trademark of Microsoft Corporation. Macintosh®
and Mac OS® are registered trademarks of Apple Computer, Inc.

This entire book has been user tested on computers with Microsoft
Office 98 Macintosh Edition installed. All figures in the book were created
from that software. Users of other versions may expect to see differences.

This book is a guide to learning and using Microsoft Office 98, not a formal
specification of the software as delivered to the buyer now or in future
software revisions. Microsoft Corporation makes no warranties with respect
to this book or to its accuracy in describing any current or future version of
Microsoft Office.

Library of Congress Cataloging-in-Publication Data

Sebastian, Bonita, 1940–
    Microsoft Office 98 step by step : Macintosh edition : word processing with Word,
  presentations with PowerPoint, spreadsheets with Excel / Bonita Sebastian
      p. cm.
    ISBN 1–57426–093–6
    1. Microsoft Office.   2. Microsoft Word   3. Microsoft Excel (Computer file)
  4. Microsoft PowerPoint (Computer file)   5. Business—Computer programs.
  6. Word processing.   7. Electronic spreadsheets.   8. Business presentations—Graphic
  methods—Computer programs.   I. Title.
  HF5548.4.m525S397   1998
  005.369—dc21   98–20089
                                                                                    CIP

Computer Literacy Press, Inc.
11584 Goldcoast Drive
Cincinnati, OH 45249

(800) 225-5413

http://www.compLitpress.com

Printed in the United States of America
10 9 8 7 6 5 4 3 2 1   90321098

Contents

Preface

Microsoft Office 98 Step by Step is based on an old Chinese proverb: "I hear, and I forget. I see, and I remember. I do, and I understand." Each page of the book is a simple list of steps for you to do at the computer. With just a little reading and a whole lot of doing, you'll quickly see how to use each of the many Office 98 tools for writing, editing, checking spelling, formatting text, printing form letters, using graphics tools to create appealing presentations, doing complex calculations, creating charts, and working with collections of data.

You need not go through the whole book from beginning to end. If you're already a Macintosh user, skip pages 1–5. Everyone should do pages 6–17. After that, either continue in order or jump to topics you're especially interested in. To help you navigate from topic to topic, icons in the upper-left corner of some pages will warn you when some previous topic or activity should have been done first. Here's a list of icons and what they mean:

 Be sure you have completed the previous topic before beginning this one.

 Make sure a document of the correct type is open before doing the first step on this page.

 Make sure your floppy disk has the named document saved on it before beginning this page.

A word of advice. Read each step carefully, do exactly what it says, watch the screen to see what happens, and go on to the next step. Sometimes you'll be tempted to go off and check out a few ideas on your own. *Don't give in to the temptation!* The result can change things in ways that make later steps in the book produce surprising results.

This is not to say exploring on your own is bad. Just the reverse—you should feel free to try anything out. Just make sure you complete a set of topics in the book, save your document if necessary, and then do all the exploration you want. When you finish, discard the document you used for experimentation.

Use mouse actions

To use the Macintosh efficiently, you need to master the mouse and the five main ways to use it.

1 **Switch on computer and monitor.**

Screen should have all features in figure. You may see others.

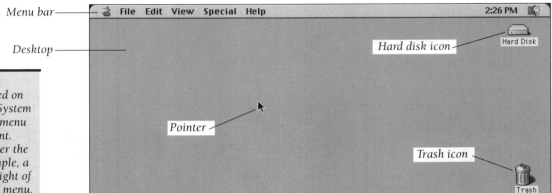

Menu bar —

Desktop —

Hard disk icon

Pointer

Trash icon

By the way

Figures in this book are based on Mac OS 8. If you are using System 7.6 or earlier, icons and the menu bar will look slightly different. Instead of the word Help after the other menu names, for example, a large question mark at the right of the menu bar heads the help menu.

2 **Move pointer:**

Hold mouse on smooth surface, wire away from you.

Watch pointer on screen as you slide mouse toward and away from you.

Watch pointer as you move mouse left and right.

Move mouse in circle. Try to move pointer off screen.

By the way

Computers can do nothing without a program. The program you'll be exploring on pages 2–5 is called the Finder. It begins running as soon as you start the computer, and it remains available until you shut down the computer.

3 **Click object to select it:**

Move pointer tip inside **Trash** icon at lower right.

Watch **Trash** icon as you tap mouse button.

4 **Press object to see more:**

Move pointer to **File** in menu bar.

Hold down mouse button to see menu.

Pressing menu name shows menu as long as you hold mouse button down.

Release mouse button.

Tip

If you're using Mac OS 8, just click a menu name to see the menu. The menu stays in view for a time, then closes automatically. You can close it manually by clicking outside the menu.

5 **Drag object to move it:**

Move pointer tip inside **Trash** icon.

Hold mouse button down as you move mouse inch or so.

Release mouse button.

6 **Double-click object:**

With pointer tip inside **Trash** icon, quickly tap mouse button twice.

This is shortcut for "opening" Trash window. It's probably empty.

Give menu commands

Macintosh applications always have a menu bar at the top of the screen. You do things by choosing commands on menus.

1 **Select Trash window:**

If stripes do not appear at top of **Trash** window, click inside window.

> *Stripes mean window is selected. Menu commands affect selected object.*

2 **Give menu command to close window (Method 1: with Mac OS 8 only):**

Click **File** in menu bar at top of screen.

Move pointer down to **Close Window** to highlight command name.

Click mouse button to choose highlighted command.

> Trash *window disappears.*

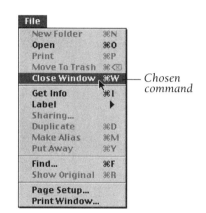

— *Chosen command*

3 **Give menu command to close window (Method 2: with System 7.6 or earlier):**

> *This method can also be used with Mac OS 8.*

Press **File** in menu bar at top of screen.

Drag pointer down to **Close Window**.

Release mouse button while command name is highlighted.

> Trash *window disappears.*

4 **Close other windows:**

Use proper method above to select and close any other open windows.

5 **Give command to get information about Trash:**

Click **Trash** icon once to select it.

Show **File** menu again (by clicking or pressing).

Move (or drag) pointer down to **Get Info**.

Click (or release) mouse button while command name is highlighted.

> *From now on in this book, steps like last three are abbreviated as follows:* "On File *menu, choose* Get Info."

6 **Close Get Info window:**

Make sure window is selected (has stripes in title bar).

On **File** menu, choose **Close Window**.

7 **Open and close Trash window again:**

If **Trash** icon is not highlighted, click it once to select it.

On **File** menu, choose **Open**.

> *You can open icon this way or by double-clicking it.*

On **File** menu, choose **Close Window**.

Explore windows

Macintosh applications always display information in windows. You control the position and size of windows.

1 **Open hard disk window:**

Double-click hard disk icon (just below right end of menu bar).

Double-clicking is shortcut for clicking icon and then giving Open *command on* File *menu.*

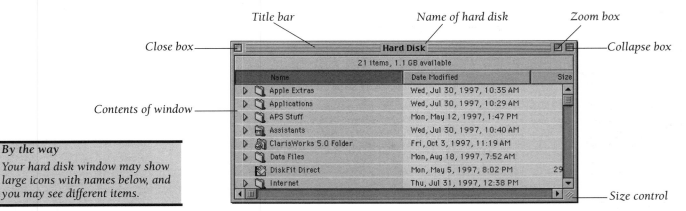

Title bar — Name of hard disk — Zoom box

Close box — Hard Disk — Collapse box

Contents of window

Size control

> **By the way**
> *Your hard disk window may show large icons with names below, and you may see different items.*

2 **Move window:**

Press stripes in title bar at top of window. Drag window to new location.

3 **Use size control:**

Press size control (lower-right corner; will look like this in System 7.6 or earlier: 🔲). Drag in any direction.

4 **Use zoom and collapse boxes:**

Click zoom box (see figure above). Click again to return to previous size.

Click collapse box, if present (see figure above), to hide contents. Click again to redisplay contents.

Collapse box lets you hide window contents without closing. Title bar remains in view. (You may also double-click title bar for same effects.)

5 **Explore two windows:**

Double-click **Trash** icon.

If necessary, drag **Trash** window so you can see part of hard disk window.

Click anywhere in hard disk window. Look at title bar.

Click anywhere in **Trash** window. Look at title bar.

Stripes in title bar show which window is selected. Commands affect selected object.

6 **Close both windows:**

Click close box (see figure above) on each window.

Clicking close box is shortcut for Close Window *command on* File *menu.*

← *Complete previous activity before going on.*

Use scroll bars

A Macintosh window may not show all the information in a document or folder. Scroll bars let you bring all parts into view.

View
as Icons
as Buttons
✓ as List
✓ as Window
as Pop-up Window
Clean Up
Sort List ▶
View Options...

By the way
Your window may contain different items and may not have shading.

1 **Open Control Panels window:**

On Apple menu (small apple at far left), choose **Control Panels**.

Control Panel *window is used here because it contains many items.*

2 **Arrange window:**

On **View** menu, choose **as List** (in System 7.6 or earlier, choose **by Name**).

Press size control (lower-right corner), and drag to make window same size as figure.

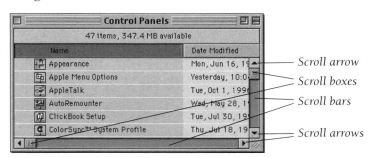

Scroll arrow
Scroll boxes
Scroll bars
Scroll arrows

3 **Use scroll arrows:**

Press scroll arrow at bottom of vertical scroll bar (at right).

Contents of window move up. Scroll box at right moves down. Scroll box stands for part of contents now in view. Gray areas in scroll bar stand for parts not in view.

Explore other scroll arrows on both scroll bars.

4 **Drag scroll box:**

Press scroll box in vertical scroll bar.

Drag slowly down or up. Release mouse button.

Text moves up or down (smoothly with Mac OS 8).

Repeat above steps with box in horizontal scroll bar.

5 **Click above or below scroll box:**

Drag scroll box to middle of vertical scroll bar.

Place pointer below box in vertical scroll bar. Click once to move down one window height.

Place pointer above box in vertical scroll bar. Click once to move up one window height.

Controls in horizontal scroll bar work same way.

6 **Close Control Panels window.**

Prepare floppy disk

*While using this book, you'll be saving all your work on a
floppy disk.*

1 *Insert floppy disk into disk drive:*

Locate blank or recycled 1.4 MB floppy disk.

Insert (slider end first, label side up) into floppy drive slot on computer.

2 *If dialog box says disk is unreadable, do these steps; if not, skip to step 3:*

If dialog box has **Initialize** button, click it. Then Click **Continue**.

OR

If dialog box has **Two-Sided** button, click it. Then click **Erase**.

> *After a minute or two, floppy disk icon appears at right edge of desktop.*

Skip to step 4.

3 *If no dialog box appears, erase disk manually:*

Click new floppy disk icon (below hard disk icon).

On **Special** menu, choose **Erase Disk**.

In dialog box, check that format is **Macintosh 1.4 MB**.

Click **Erase** button to erase everything on disk.

> *Erasing and verifying disk takes a minute or two.*

4 *Name floppy disk:*

Click name box under new floppy disk icon at right edge of desktop.

Wait for line to form around highlighted name.

Type **Work Disk**.

5 *Remove floppy disk this way:*

Press pointer on **Work Disk** floppy disk icon.

Drag icon in front of **Trash** icon.

When **Trash** icon is highlighted, release mouse button.

> *Disk pops from drive. You did not lose anything; this is how to eject disk.*

Remove floppy disk, label it "Work Disk," and store it safely for future use.

6 *Shut down computer:*

Click clear area of desktop (to make sure Finder is active).

On **Special** menu, choose **Shut Down**.

If asked, switch off computer and monitor.

Start Office application

You're now ready to start a Microsoft Office application running on your Macintosh.

1 **Switch on computer and monitor if necessary.**

2 **Locate Microsoft Office 98 folder:**

Double-click hard disk icon.

Find Microsoft Office 98 folder.

> *It may be inside another folder. If you see a folder named Applications, Programs, or Software, open it and look there. (Also, see tip at left.)*

> **Tip**
> *Your computer may have shortcuts, depending on your system. Use the Apple menu at the left to choose* Recent Applications, *then choose* Word, PowerPoint, *or* Excel. *Or, if you see the* proper *icon in the* Launcher *window, just click it.*

3 **Locate applications:**

Double-click Microsoft Office 98 folder.

> *Icons at top of figure below stand for applications you'll study in this book. (Icons may be smaller, and names may appear in list.)*

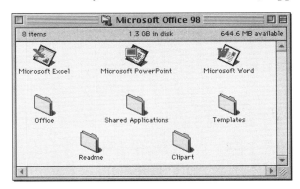

4 **Start Microsoft Office application:**

> *For now, you'll start Microsoft Word. Method is same for all.*

Double-click **Microsoft Word** icon (or name in list).

> *In time, screen changes to figure similar to one below.*

Menu bar for Microsoft Word ——
Standard toolbar ——
Formatting toolbar ——
Title bar ——

Finder desktop ——

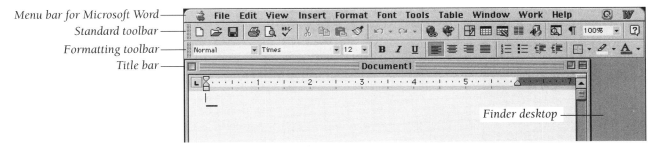

If **Office Assistant** window appears, click **Start using Microsoft Word**. Then click close box on same window.

> *Notice that you can see part of Finder desktop to right of document window. Finder application is still running, as you'll see soon.*

5 **Quit application:**

On **File** menu, choose **Quit**.

Use application menu

With two applications running at the same time, switching between them by accident is common. Here's the remedy.

1 Start Microsoft Word application (see page 7):

Look at application icon (at right end of menu bar).

 —— *Application icon for Microsoft Word*

Icon shape shows that Microsoft Word is active application.

2 Switch applications by accident:

Click close box on **Document 1** window.

Look at icons and windows on desktop.

> *They were there when you started Microsoft Word. They don't belong to Word, but you might click one by accident.*

Click anywhere on desktop. Look at menu bar. Look at application icon.

 —— *Application icon for Finder (Mac OS 8)* —— *Application icon for Finder (System 7.6)*

> *Icon shape means Finder is active application. (Finder runs as soon as you start computer. Finder displays desktop icons and has menus you now see.)*

3 Use application menu to switch back to Microsoft Word:

Click (or press) application icon.

> *Check mark shows Finder is active application.*

On application menu, choose **Microsoft Word**.

Look at application icon now.

> *Icon tells you Microsoft Word is active again.*

4 Avoid accidental window clicks:

Make sure application icon is for Microsoft Word.

On application menu, choose **Hide Others**.

> *Finder windows disappear. Now there's no temptation to click one. (But clicking desktop, disk icon, or Trash icon still makes Finder active!)*

5 End session at computer:

On **File** menu, choose **Quit**.

If **Microsoft Office Folder** window is open, click close box at upper left.

On **Special** menu, choose **Shut Down**.

> **Tip**
> *When the computer isn't working the way it should, your first step should be to check the application icon and see what is active.*

Start Microsoft Word

You are now ready to start the Microsoft Word application running on your computer.

1 **Start computer and Word:**

Switch on computer (see page 2).

Start Microsoft Word (see page 7).

If **Office Assistant** window appears, click **Start using Microsoft Word**, then click ▣ (close box) to shut window.

2 **View document window for Word.**

Screen should appears as in figure, with document name in title bar.

Menu bar —
Standard toolbar —
Formatting toolbar —
Title bar —
Ruler —
Place to enter text —

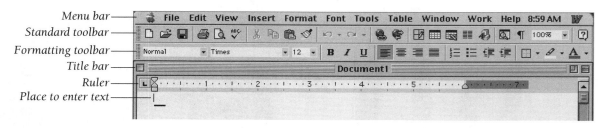

If necessary, use commands on View menu to show and hide toolbars and ruler. You may also widen window as shown in figure.

3 **Observe tools on toolbars:**

Place pointer over any icon on either toolbar.

Name of tool appears below pointer.

> **By the way**
> *Toolbar icons are shortcuts for often-used menu commands. You get the same result whether you click the toolbar icon or choose the same command from a menu.*

4 **Set view options:**

On **Tools** menu, choose **Preferences**.

You can set dozens of options that change the way Word appears and works. You'll make a few helpful settings now.

If necessary, click **View** tab to bring its page to front.

In **Nonprinting characters** area of dialog box, click **All** (if necessary) to put mark in check box.

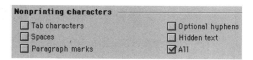

Special symbols will appear in text to show characters that are normally invisible: spaces, paragraph marks, and tabs. By making them visible, you'll see how they work and you'll avoid deleting one by accident.

Click **OK**.

Now you're ready to enter text in new document.

Create new document

Entering text into a new document is usually the first step in using a word processor program.

1 Observe insertion point:

Look for small blinking vertical line to left of paragraph mark.

Insertion point is where characters will appear when you type.

2 Enter text:

Type following text. Do *not* tap RETURN at ends of lines.

> **Thank you for your interest in our flower subscription service. When you become one of our subscribers, you'll never have to worry about forgetting an important date again!**

Insertion point moves as you enter text. Notice words in paragraph automatically "wrap" (continue on next line when end of line is reached).

Tap RETURN now.

RETURN *is at right of main group of keys.*

Look at insertion point and new paragraph mark.

Tapping RETURN *marks end of paragraph and moves insertion point to next line. Space characters appear as small centered dots.*

3 Enter more text:

Tap RETURN again to create blank line.

Another end-of-paragraph mark is visible on blank line.

Type following text. Don't worry about typing errors now. You'll fix them later.

> **We ship the freshest and most beautiful flowers and plants to any home or business address in North America. Subscriptions are available for daily, monthly, quarterly, or yearly delivery. We can even customize a schedule especially for you.**

Tap RETURN twice.

Type following text. Don't worry about typing errors now. You'll fix them later.

> **I am enclosing a brochure describing our services in detail. If you have any questions, please do not hesitate to call me.**

Tap RETURN twice.

Tip

Type just one space between your sentences. Typing two spaces is an old habit left over from the days of using a typewriter with fixed-width characters. The period was in the middle of a wide space, so extra space after it helped show that a new sentence was beginning.

By the way

If you type a phrase Microsoft Word recognizes, you may see an information box appear. To learn more about this feature, see page 43.

> Thank you,
> Thank ¶

If you make a spelling mistake while typing, Microsoft Word may put a red zig zag line under the word: hesitate to*. Don't worry about spelling mistakes. You will correct them later.*

4　*Use these steps to correct any error:*

Move I-beam pointer just right of error, then click.

> *Insertion point appears where you clicked.*

Tap DELETE one or more times to remove characters.

> *Delete key is at upper-right corner of main group of keys.*

Retype to enter correct characters.

Finished document should look like this:

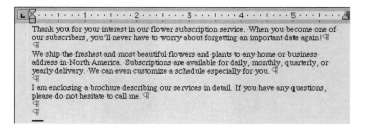

Tip
You can also move the insertion
point through a document using the
four arrow keys to the right of the
main group of keys.

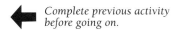 *Complete previous activity before going on.*

Save document

After creating and editing a new document, you should save it on a disk.

1 **Insert floppy disk:**

Insert disk, slider end first, label side up, into floppy drive.

2 **Give Save command:**

On **File** menu, choose **Save** (or click 🖫 on standard toolbar).

> Save As *dialog box appears on first use of* Save *command. You must name document and say where to save it.*

3 **Name document:**

Note suggested name is highlighted in **Save Current Document as** text box at bottom.

Type **Letter** in text box. Use `DELETE` to erase errors.

> *Typed characters replace highlighted text.*

4 **Say where to save document:**

Click [**Desktop**] (desktop button) at right of dialog.

Double-click 🖫 **Work Disk** (floppy disk icon) on list in center of dialog box.

Save As dialog box should look like figure below.

Location where you want document saved ⎯

Name of document ⎯

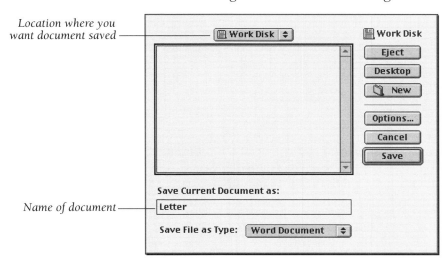

Click **Save** to save document with name **Letter** on floppy disk.

> *Document is copied to disk. When copying is finished, new document name appears in title bar.*

5 **Add to document and save again:**

Click to left of last paragraph mark.

Type **Sincerely,** then tap `RETURN` three times, and type your name.

On **File** menu, choose **Save** (or click 🖫 on standard toolbar).

By the way

No dialog box appears this time. The changed file takes place of the original on the floppy disk. The original is permanently erased!

Save with new name

Often you need to save a changed document with a new name or in a new location so it won't erase the original.

1 **Add more text to document:**

Click at end of your name.

Tap [RETURN] twice.

Type following postscript:

> **P.S. We are offering a special of 10% off for new customers through the end of the month. Please call right away to take advantage of this special offer.**

2 **Save changed document without erasing original:**

On **File** menu, choose **Save As** (*not* Save).

> *Save As dialog box shows current name and location of document. You can change either or both.*

Type **Promo** as name for changed document.

Leave location as [Work Disk ⬦] (floppy disk).

Click **Save** button.

> *You now have two documents on floppy disk. Letter has original text. Promo has original plus postscript.*

Look at title bar on document window.

> *Title bar now has new document name. If you use Save command now, only new document is affected.*

3 **Close Promo document:**

On **File** menu, choose **Close**.

> *If you hadn't just saved your changes, Microsoft Word would have asked whether you wanted to save them before closing. Answering Yes is same as giving Save command. Answering No discards changes. Answering Cancel stops Close command and returns to document.*

Look at screen.

> *Only menu bar and toolbars remain. Microsoft Word application is still open. No Microsoft Word document is open now.*

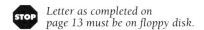 *Letter as completed on page 13 must be on floppy disk.*

Open saved document

After saving a document on a disk, you must open it from the disk to continue work.

1 *Prepare to open document on floppy disk:*

> *In this exercise, you'll open* Letter.

If floppy disk is not in drive, insert it now.

On **File** menu, choose **Open** (or click ⬚ on standard toolbar).

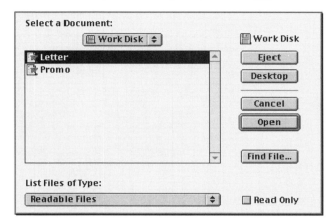

> Open *is like* Save As *dialog box. Files* Letter *and* Promo *should appear in center.* Readable Files *should appear on pop-up menu at bottom.*

2 *Say what drive contains disk:*

If dialog box does not look like figure, click **Desktop** button.

Then double-click |⬚ **Work Disk** (floppy disk icon).

3 *Open file you want:*

Click **Letter** to select it as document to open. Then click **Open**.

OR

Double-click **Letter**.

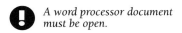

A word processor document must be open.

Print document

As you work on a word processor document, you often need to print a copy to take away, read, and correct.

1 *Check paper size:*

On **File** menu, choose **Page Setup**.

If necessary, select **Page Attributes** from pop-up list at upper left of dialog box.

> *Your* Page Setup *and* Print *dialog boxes may look slightly different.*

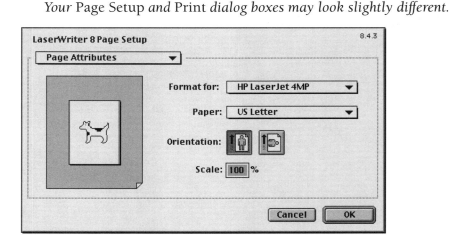

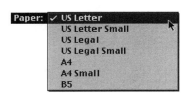

View **Paper** size list, then select size of paper used in your printer.

2 *Choose orientation of printed image on page.*

3 *Choose Scale.*

4 *Click OK to accept page setup choices.*

5 *Check printer.*

> *Is printer plugged in and is switch on? If printer has On light or Select light, is it on? Is paper in tray?*

6 *Open Print dialog box:*

On **File** menu, choose **Print**.

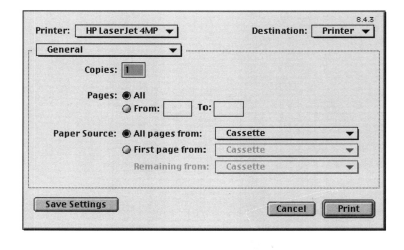

7 *Note standard settings:*

Note **Printer** name. Make sure it is one you want to use.

If not, click or press ▼ and select printer from list.

8 *Specify number of copies (in this exercise, use 1):*

Verify that **Copies** says number you want.

OR

Click inside **Copies** box and type number you want.

9 *Choose range of pages:*

On pop-up list below printer list, choose **Microsoft Word**.

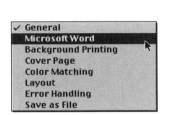

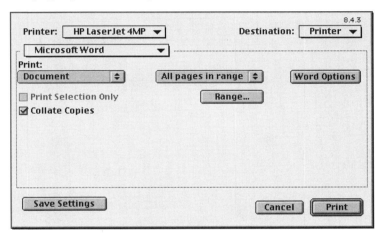

For this example, choose **All pages in range**.

10 *Send document to printer, or cancel:*

Click **Print** button.

If you don't want to print, click **Cancel** button instead.

11 *Close Letter document without saving changes:*

On **File** menu, choose **Close**.

If this dialog box appears, click **Don't Save**.

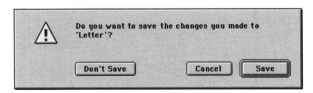

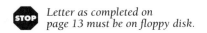
Find text

You can get help in finding words you're looking for—a nice feature if your document has lots of text.

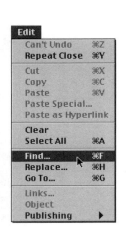

1 **Open Letter document.**

    See page 15 for details.

2 **Find word:**

On **Edit** menu, choose **Find**.

Type **You** in **Find what** box.

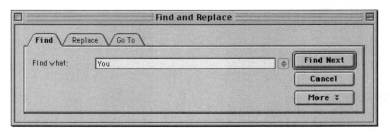

Click **Find Next** until search ends.

    You *appears six times before search ends. Note that* you *in* your *and in* you'll *were also found. (You may have to move dialog box to see text.)*

Click **OK** to close dialog box that reports end of search.

3 **Find whole word:**

Click **More** button to see additional options.

In **Search** section, click **Find whole words only** to put mark in check box.

Click **Find Next** until search ends. Click **OK**.

    You *appears only five times because you asked for only that word and not others that contain those letters (except with an apostrophe as in* you'll*).*

Tip

The Find *command is especially useful in long documents. It allows you to go directly to words or phrases anywhere in a document.*

4 **Make case-sensitive search:**

In **Search** section, click **Match case** to put mark in check box.

Click **Find Next**.

    You *with first letter capitalized is not found anywhere.*

Click **OK**.

5 **Click Cancel button to end Find.**

Complete previous activity before going on.

Replace text

Sometimes you need to change one word to another in many places in a document.

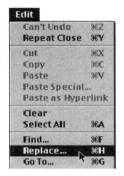

By the way
Notice that the last search text appears highlighted in the Find what box, and check boxes are the way you left them.

1 *Begin replacement:*

Put insertion point at start of document.

On **Edit** menu, choose **Replace**.

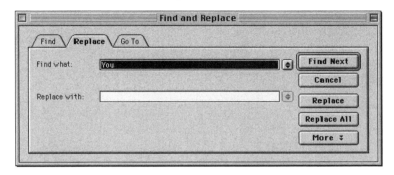

2 *Enter text to be replaced:*

Type **flower**. Tap TAB to move to **Replace with** box.

Type **bonsai**.

Click **More** button if necessary.

Click **Match case** and **Find whole words only** to remove marks.

3 *Find and replace words one a time:*

Click **Find Next**.

First occurrence of flower *in document is highlighted.*

Click **Replace**.

Flower is replaced by bonsai *and next occurrence is highlighted. This is word* flowers, *which you don't want to change at this time.*

Click **Find Next**.

There are no more occurrences.

Click **OK** to close message box.

4 *Find and replace words without checking:*

Click to right of **flower** in **Find what** text box.

Type **s** and click **Replace All**.

Only one instance of word flowers *is changed to* bonsai.

5 *End Replace:*

Click **OK** and then click **Close** button.

6 *Close Letter document without saving changes.*

STOP *Letter as completed on
page 13 must be on floppy disk.*

Check spelling

*Microsoft Word can check the spelling in a document and add
new words to your custom dictionary.*

1 Open Letter document:

See page 15 for details.

OR

Choose **Letter** in bottom section of **File** menu.

> **By the way**
> *You may see a red zig zag line under
> misspelled words. You can switch
> this feature off. Go to* Tools, *then*
> Preferences, *then* Spelling &
> Grammar.

2 Create spelling errors in paragraph 1:

Change *subscription* to *suscription.* Change *become* to *becume.*

Change *forgetting* to *forgeting.* Change *important* to *importent.*

3 Position insertion point:

Put insertion point at top of document.

> *If text in document is selected, Microsoft Word will check that text only.*

4 Open Spelling dialog box:

On **Tools** menu, choose **Spelling and Grammar**.

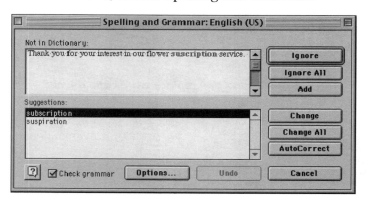

> **By the way**
> *If a dialog box appears asking to
> create a custom dictionary, click* Yes.

5 Correct first misspelled word:

> *Correct spelling of* subscription *is highlighted in* Suggestions *list.*

Click **Change**.

> *You may get warnings about grammar during spelling check. If so, close
> information box and go on.*

6 Correct second misspelled word:

Two possible correct spellings appear.

Click to select **become**, then click **Change**.

7 *Correct other misspelled words:*

Use one of methods in step 5 or 6 on previous page to correct two other misspelled words.

If you find additional "typos," correct them as well.

By the way

If you've corrected all errors, the dialog box closes and you won't be able to add a word to the dictionary.

8 *Add unknown word to dictionary:*

Last word(s) flagged by spelling checker may be your name. You can add word(s) to dictionary to prevent flagging in future.

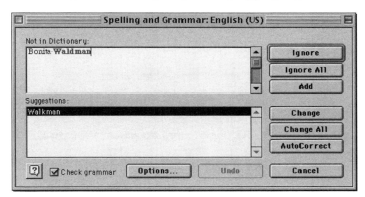

Click **Add** to add word to dictionary.

Microsoft Word automatically adds word to custom dictionary, which is shared with Microsoft Excel and Microsoft PowerPoint.

Spelling-check-complete message box appears.

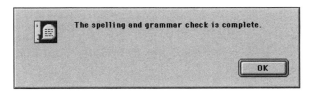

You may see a Readability Statistics report. If so, close box and go on.

9 *Close spelling checker:*

Click **OK**.

10 *Close Letter without saving changes:*

On **File** menu, choose **Close**.

Click **Don't Save** when asked whether to save changes.

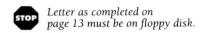

Highlight text

Text must be highlighted before you can make changes in font, size, style, and the like.

1 Open Letter document:

See page 15 for details.

OR

Select **Letter** in bottom section of **File** menu.

2 Highlight entire document (method 1):

On **Edit** menu, choose **Select All** (or hold down ⌘ and tap Ⓐ).

> *There are two ⌘ keys—one on each side of spacebar. Other menu commands often have "command key" shortcuts like this. (Hereafter, key combinations like this will appear as ⌘ Ⓐ.)*

3 Deselect highlighted area:

Click anywhere in text.

4 Highlight entire document (method 2):

Position pointer on left side of document.

Watch for pointer shape to change to arrow pointing up and to right.

Triple-click mouse button.

Click anywhere in text to deselect it.

5 Highlight many lines of document:

Position pointer to left of first line you want to select.

> *Pointer shape changes to arrow pointing up and to right.*

Press mouse button and drag pointer down left side of document.

> *Highlighting follows pointer.*

Release mouse button.

Click anywhere in text to deselect highlighted area.

6 Highlight block of text (method 1):

Position I-beam pointer before first letter you want to select.

Press and hold mouse button and drag pointer through text you want to select.

> *End of selection can be on same or different line.*

Release mouse button.

7   *Highlight block of text (method 2):*

Position I-beam pointer to left of first word you want to select.

Click to place insertion point.

Hold down `SHIFT`.

Click to put insertion point after last word you want to select.

Release `SHIFT`.

> *All text between places you clicked is highlighted.*

8   *Add to selected text:*

Hold down `SHIFT`.

Click to put insertion point after new last word you want to select.

Release `SHIFT`.

> *All text between last two places you clicked is added to selection.*

9   *Highlight one word:*

Double-click any word.

> *Note that space after word is also highlighted.*

10   *Highlight one sentence:*

Hold down `⌘`.

Click anywhere in sentence.

> *Entire sentence including period and space(s) after are highlighted.*

11   *Highlight paragraph:*

Triple-click anywhere in paragraph.

OR

Position pointer to left of paragraph you want to select.

> *Pointer shape changes to arrow pointing up and to right.*

Double-click.

12   *Deselect highlighted area:*

Click anywhere in text.

> *Text is no longer highlighted, and insertion point is positioned where you last clicked.*

By the way

Microsoft Word is normally set up to select whole words, even if you click inside a word instead of clicking just before or after it.

Tip

You can add text only in the same direction as before. You can remove text by clicking after the last letter you want to remain in selection.

Cut, copy, paste & clear

*After entering text, you often need to erase parts of it and move
sentences and paragraphs around.*

1 *Highlight paragraph 2:*

Position pointer to left of paragraph 2.

Press and drag pointer down. Also select blank line after paragraph.

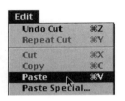

2 *Move paragraph 2 ahead of paragraph 1:*

On **Edit** menu, choose **Cut** (or tap ⌘ X, or click ✂ on standard toolbar)
to remove highlighted text.

Click before first word in paragraph 1.

> *Blinking insertion point shows where cut text will be inserted. (If whole line
> is accidentally highlighted, repeat above step.)*

On **Edit** menu, choose **Paste** (or tap ⌘ V, or click 📋 on standard
toolbar) to insert text you just cut.

> *Former paragraph 2 is now paragraph 1.*

3 *Place copy of paragraph 3 ahead of new paragraph 1:*

Highlight paragraph 3 and blank line after it.

On **Edit** menu, choose **Copy** (or tap ⌘ C, or click 📋 on standard
toolbar) to copy highlighted text.

Click before first word in paragraph 1.

On **Edit** menu, choose **Paste** (or tap ⌘ V, or click 📋 on standard
toolbar) to insert text you just copied.

> *Former paragraph 3 now appears twice in document.*

4 *Delete new paragraph 1:*

Highlight paragraph 1. Include blank line after it.

On **Edit** menu, choose **Clear** (or tap DELETE) to delete highlighted text.

5 *Add word:*

Click before any word in any paragraph.

Type **new** and tap SPACEBAR.

> *Note that Microsoft Word capitalizes new first character.*

6 *Delete word:*

Double-click word **new**.

> *Word and space after it are highlighted.*

Tap DELETE.

> *Word and extra space disappear.*

7 *Close Letter without saving changes.*

STOP *Letter as completed on page 13 must be on floppy disk.*

Use drag & drop editing

Here's another way to move and duplicate text in a document. Many people find it simpler and more direct.

1 **Open Letter document.**

2 **Highlight paragraph 2:**

Position pointer to left of paragraph 2.

Press and drag pointer down. Also select blank line after paragraph.

3 **Move paragraph 2 ahead of paragraph 1:**

Notice pointer shape as you move it into any highlighted text.

Pointer changes from I-beam to arrow.

With pointer in highlighted text, hold down mouse button.

Drag arrow pointer just before first word in paragraph 1. Notice that dotted insertion point moves with arrow.

Release mouse button.

Highlighted text disappears from old location and is inserted at arrow position. You have dragged paragraph 2 and dropped it before paragraph 1.

4 **Place copy of paragraph 3 ahead of new paragraph 1:**

Highlight paragraph 3 and blank line after it.

Put pointer in highlighted text.

Hold down OPTION and mouse button.

Drag arrow pointer just before first word in new paragraph 1.

Release mouse button first, then OPTION.

You've dragged copy of paragraph 3 and dropped it before paragraph 1.

5 **Close Letter without saving changes:**

On **File** menu, choose **Close**.

Click **Don't Save** in dialog box.

Undo changes

Microsoft Word allows you to undo actions you have performed to change content or format of document.

1 **Open Letter document.**

2 **Select paragraph 1:**

Position pointer to left of paragraph 1.

> *Pointer shape changes to this:*

Double-click.

3 **Delete paragraph:**

Tap (DELETE).

> *Paragraph is deleted.*

4 **Undo action (method 1):**

On **Edit** menu, choose **Undo Typing** (or tap ⌘ Z).

> *Paragraph is "undeleted."*

5 **Delete paragraph again:**

Select paragraph if necessary, and tap (DELETE).

> *Paragraph is again deleted.*

6 **Undo action (method 2):**

Click or press left part of ↶▾ (undo tool) on standard toolbar.

> *Paragraph is again "undeleted."*

7 **Undo multiple actions:**

Click anywhere in paragraph 1 and type **AAAA**.

Click anywhere in paragraph 2 and type **BBBB**.

Click anywhere in paragraph 3 and type **CCCC**.

Click or press arrow on right part of ↶▾ (undo tool).

> *List shows changes you've made. Most recent is at top and rest are in order.*

On undo list, choose **Typing "AAAA"**.

> *Three most recent changes are undone.*

8 **Redo changes just undone:**

On **Edit** menu, choose **Redo Typing** (or tap ⌘ Y).

> *You should again see AAAA in paragraph 1.*

Repeat twice more to see other changes reappear.

9 **Close document without saving changes.**

STOP *Letter as completed on page 13 must be on floppy disk.*

Change fonts & font sizes

Text can appear in many different fonts and sizes. Each font specifies the shapes of all the letters, numbers, and symbols.

1 **Open Letter document.**

2 **Check current font and size of text in paragraph 1:**

Highlight any text in paragraph 1.

On formatting toolbar, look at font name and size.

Toolbar shows name and size of font used for selected text.

3 **Change font (method 1):**

On formatting toolbar, click or press ▾ next to font name to see font list.

Your list of fonts may be different.

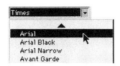

On font list, choose **Arial**.

Menu command only affects highlighted text.

4 **Change font (method 2):**

Highlight any text in paragraph 2.

On **Font** menu, choose **Apple Chancery**. (If not available, use other font of your choice.)

5 **Change size:**

On formatting toolbar, click or press ▾ next to current size to see font size list.

Choose **18**.

6 **Change font and size:**

On font list, choose **Courier**. (If not available, use other of your choice.)

On font size list, choose **9**.

7 **Change fonts and sizes, and save results:**

Give words in each paragraph different fonts and sizes.

On **File** menu, choose **Save As** (*not* Save).

Type **Fonts** in Save Current Document as box.

Click **Save**.

Changed document is saved with new name. Original remains unchanged.

Apply font styles

You can easily add font styles, such as bold or italic, to selected words in the document.

1 **Add single style to all text in paragraph 2:**

Highlight all of paragraph 2.

On formatting toolbar, click **B** (bold tool) or tap ⌘ B.

> *Paragraph 2 appears in bold type. Note bold tool is darker and recessed.*

2 **Remove same style:**

On formatting toolbar, click **B** again, or tap ⌘ B again.

> *Command is like off/on switch, so bold style is removed when you choose command again. Dark highlight on tool tells when it is on.*

3 **Add styles one at a time:**

Paragraph 2 should still be selected. If not, select it now.

On formatting toolbar, click **B** or tap ⌘ B.

On formatting toolbar, click **I** (italic tool) or tap ⌘ I.

On formatting toolbar, click **U** (underline tool) or tap ⌘ U.

> *All three tools now have light highlight.*

Click outside paragraph 2 to deselect text and see styles.

> *Tools no longer have light highlight. That's because insertion point is not in paragraph 2 now.*

4 **Remove added styles one at a time:**

Select all text in paragraph 2.

Watch text as you click **B**, then **I**, then **U** .

5 **Undo removal of styles:**

Click or press arrow on right part of ↺ ▾ (undo tool).

On undo list, choose *first* occurrence of **Bold**.

> *All three styles are added back to text.*

6 **Return whole paragraph to default font, font size, and style:**

Select all text in paragraph 2. Tap ⌘ SHIFT Z.

7 **Apply font styles, save, and close document:**

Apply a different font style to words in each paragraph of document.

On **File** menu, choose **Save As** (*not* Save).

Type **Styles** in Save Current Document as box. Click **Save**.

> *Changed document is saved with new name. Original remains unchanged.*

On **File** menu, choose **Close**.

Use Font dialog box

A single dialog box lets you specify all character formats at the same time: the font, the size, the styles, and other details.

1 **Open Letter document.**

2 **Change font, size, style, and color at same time:**

Highlight all text in paragraph 1.

On **Format** menu, choose **Font**.

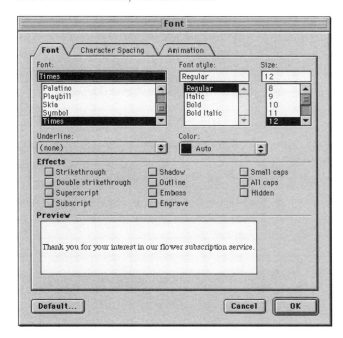

If dialog box does not look like this, click Font *tab.*

Use scroll bars on **Font** list to see fonts. Click to highlight one you want.

On **Font style** list, click **Bold Italic**.

Use scroll bars on **Size** list to see sizes. Click to highlight one you want.

On **Underline** list, choose **Single**. On **Color** list, choose **Red**.

In **Effects** area, click **All caps** to put mark in check box.

Click **OK**. Then click away from paragraph 1 to see result.

All changes happen at same time.

3 **Remove all character formats:**

You could do this with Fonts *dialog box, but there's an easier way.*

Highlight all text in paragraph 1. Tap ⌘ SHIFT Z.

4 **Close document without saving changes:**

On **File** menu, choose **Close**.

When asked whether to save changes, click **Don't Save**.

By the way
On this list, Regular means no italic and no bold.

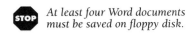
Open multiple documents

As with most Macintosh applications, you can have several documents open at the same time, but in separate windows.

1 *Open multiple documents:*

> *If floppy is not in drive, insert it now.*

On **File** menu, choose **Open**.

Click name of first document in list.

Click **Open**.

Repeat process to open all four documents.

> *All documents open, but only last document is visible.*

2 *Switch from document to document:*

On **Window** menu, choose name of document you want.

> *Because document windows are maximized, only one is visible at a time.*

3 *View all documents at one time:*

On **Window** menu, choose **Arrange All**.

> *Document windows no longer fill screen. You see separate document windows with individual title bars. Only one is active.*

4 *Switch from document to document:*

Click anywhere in window of document you want to activate.

5 *View one of four documents on full screen:*

Click any window to make it active.

Click 🔲 (zoom box) in or near upper-right corner of active window.

> *Window fills screen.*

Click 🔲 again.

> *Window returns to original size.*

Click zoom box on another document window.

> *Window fills screen.*

By the way
The other box 🔲 at the upper-right corner of the window is the collapse box (new in Mac OS 8). Clicking it collapses the window down to the title bar only.

6 *Close multiple documents:*

Press (SHIFT) and hold it down.

On **File** menu, choose **Close All**.

If asked, don't save changes.

7 *Quit Microsoft Word:*

On **File** menu, choose **Quit**.

Align text

The lines of text in a paragraph can all be aligned to the left, the right, the center, or both left and right (justified).

1 **Open new document (unless you just started Word):**

> *If you just started Word, ignore this step. Word begins with new document.*

On standard toolbar, click ▯ (new tool).

2 **Observe alignment tools on formatting toolbar:**

3 **Enter text using alignment options:**

Click ▤ (center tool).

> *Insertion point moves to center of document.*

Type **Petal Pushers Flower Shop**.

Tap RETURN twice.

> *Each new line picks up previous center alignment formatting.*

Click ▤ (align right tool).

> *Insertion point moves to right side of document.*

4 **Enter automatic date:**

On **Insert** menu, choose **Date and Time**.

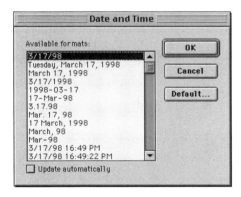

Choose format you like, then click **OK**.

5 **Enter additional text with left alignment:**

Tap RETURN twice.

> *Each new line picks up previous right alignment formatting.*

Click ▤ (align left tool).

> *Insertion point moves to left side of document.*

Type **Mr. John Smith**.

Tap RETURN twice.

> *Each new line picks up previous left alignment formatting.*

6 *Use justified alignment:*

Click ▤ (justify tool).

Type following paragraph. Do not tap RETURN at end of line. Let text wrap.

> **How many times have you forgotten an important birthday or anniversary? Let us eliminate that worry from your life! Petal Pushers Flower Subscription Service celebrates all those special dates for you with an on—time delivery of exquisite flowers or plants.**

Text in your document has even (justified) margins.

7 *Check spelling:*

On **Tools** menu, choose **Spelling and Grammar**.

See method beginning on page 20 for details.

8 *Save document:*

Make sure floppy disk is in drive.

On **File** menu, choose **Save**.

In **Save Current Document as** text box, type **Opening**.

For location, choose ▤ Work Disk ⬍ .

Click **Save**.

New document is saved on floppy disk.

9 *Move insertion point to top of document:*

Tap ⌘ HOME .

Finished document looks like figure.

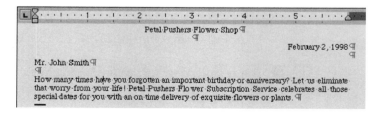

Complete previous activity before going on.

Apply indents

Other paragraph format controls let you indent lines in paragraphs from the left and right margins.

---

1 **View indent markers at ends of ruler.**

If ruler is not present, choose Ruler *on* View *menu.*

First-line indent — Left indent —  — Right indent

2 **Set right and left indents:**

Click anywhere inside justified paragraph.

Paragraph formatting applies to paragraph where insertion point is located. You don't have to highlight entire paragraph.

Press and drag right indent marker 2 inches to left (to 4" mark on ruler).

Text is indented from right margin. Only selected paragraph (one with insertion point in it) is indented. To set indents in more than one paragraph, highlight some text in each.

Press and drag rectangle *under* left indent marker 1 inch to right (to 1" mark on ruler).

Dragging rectangle moves both first-line indent marker and left indent marker.

3 **Set first-line indent:**

Carefully press and drag first-line indent marker (*top* triangle, now above left indent marker) to right one-half inch (to 1.5" mark).

This time, first line of selected paragraph is indented more than rest.

4 **Set hanging indent:**

Carefully press and drag first-line indent marker (*top* triangle) to left one inch (to 0.5" mark).

This time, first line "hangs"—begins to left of other lines. Format is useful for numbered paragraphs.

5 **Reset indents to original settings:**

If necessary, click in justified paragraph again.

Press and drag right indent marker to 6" mark on ruler.

Press and drag first-line indent marker back to left indent marker.

Press and drag rectangle *under* left indent marker to 0" mark on ruler.

Be sure to use bottom rectangle to drag triangles together.

Warning

Be careful not to drag too far to the left and into the "minus area." If this happens, use the horizontal scroll bar to see the markers.

Apply line spacing

Additional paragraph format controls let you change vertical line spacing.

1 **Double-space paragraph lines:**

If necessary, click inside justified paragraph.

> *Like alignment and indentation, line spacing affects only paragraph with insertion point (or paragraphs with some text highlighted).*

Tap ⌘ 2.

> *Lines are double-spaced now.*

2 **Single-space lines again:**

Tap ⌘ 1.

3 **Set paragraph line spacing to 1.5 lines:**

Tap ⌘ 5.

> *Paragraph lines spread apart, but less than with double-spacing.*

4 **Add space before paragraph:**

Tap ⌘ 1 to restore single-spacing.

Put insertion point at start of justified paragraph.

Tap DELETE to delete any blank lines before paragraph.

> *Now you'll learn another way to put space between paragraphs.*

Click inside justified paragraph.

Tap ⌘ 0 (zero).

> *One line space is added before selected paragraph. Notice that there's no paragraph mark on blank line.*

Double-click arrow pointer just left of justified paragraph to select it.

> *Blank line is also selected. It is part of justified paragraph.*

5 **Remove space before paragraph:**

With justified paragraph still selected, tap ⌘ 0 (zero) again.

6 **Close document without saving changes.**

Use Paragraph dialog box

Like the Font dialog box, this one lets you make many format changes at the same time. They affect whole paragraphs.

1 **Open Letter document.**

2 **Delete blank lines between paragraphs:**

Move pointer to left side of document.

Pointer changes to arrow pointing up and to right.

Click to left of first blank line after paragraph 1.

Tap (DELETE). Blank line is deleted.

Do same for blank lines after paragraphs 2 and 3 (but not after *Sincerely,*).

3 **Select some text in all three paragraphs:**

Click anywhere in paragraph 1.

With (SHIFT) held down, click anywhere in paragraph 3.

4 **Open Paragraph dialog box:**

On **Format** menu, choose **Paragraph**.

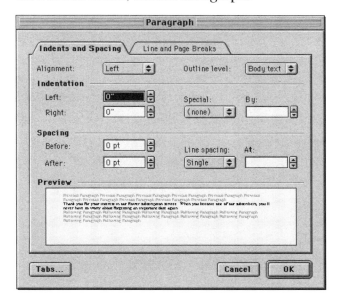

On **Special** list (in **Indentation** area), choose **First line**.

On **By** list, choose **0.5"** if necessary.

In **After** box (in **Spacing** area), click up-arrow twice to choose **12 pt**.

On **Line spacing** list, choose **1.5 lines**.

On **Alignment** list, choose **Justified**.

Click **OK**.

All format changes happen at once. Only paragraphs 1–3 are affected.

5 **Close Letter document without saving changes.**

Use tab stops

Tab stops are another paragraph format feature. They give you
control over alignment of words in columns.

1 **Open new document (unless you just started Word):**

If you just started Word, ignore this step. Word begins with new document.

On standard toolbar, click 🗋 (new tool).

2 **Note tab features on ruler:**

If ruler is not present, choose Ruler *on View menu.*

Tab stop tool ———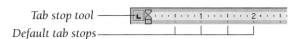
Default tab stops ———

Default tab stops every half inch are in effect until you place your own stops.

Click tab stop tool to rotate through four different stops you can set—
⊾ left, ⊥ center, ⊿ right, and ⊥ decimal.

3 **Set custom tab stops on ruler (method 1):**

Make sure tab stop tool is set to ⊾ *(left).*

Click ruler at 0.75" mark.

Left tab stop appears at 0.75" mark on ruler.

Note that default tab stop to left of custom tab disappears. Default stops to
right remain.

Click tab stop tool twice to select ⊿ (right tab stop).

Click ruler at 2.5 inches.

Use same steps to set decimal tab at 3.5 inches and center tab at 5 inches.

Ruler should look like this:

4 **Use tab stops:**

Use steps below to enter following text:

Left	Right	3.0	Center
Roses	Pansies	$1.98	Tulips

Before typing each word or number in figure, tap ⌗TAB⌗ (at left side of
keyboard).

Tap ⌗RETURN⌗ at end of each line.

You see arrow each place you tap ⌗TAB⌗. *(If not, see step 4 on page 10 to make*
nonprinting characters visible.)

5 *Clear all tab stops from new paragraph:*

Tap RETURN to skip another line.

> *Note same tab stops are in effect for new paragraph. New paragraph always "inherits" all formats from previous paragraph.*

Press and drag left tab stop (at 0.75 inches) down from ruler. Release mouse button.

Do same for other tab stops on ruler.

> *New line has default tab stops, but no custom tab stops. Custom tab stops remain in paragraphs above. Each paragraph can have own tab settings.*

6 *Set tab stops using dialog box (method 2):*

On **Format** menu, choose **Tabs**.

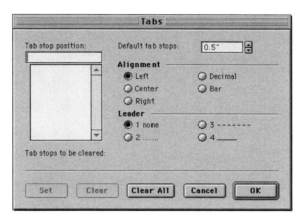

In **Tap stop position** box, type **1**.

Click **Set**.

In **Tap stop position** box, type **5**.

In **Alignment** area, click **Decimal**.

Click **Set**, then click **OK**.

7 *Use tab stops:*

Tap TAB, type **Daisies**.

Tap TAB, type **2.59**, then tap RETURN.

Tap TAB, type **Roses**.

Tap TAB, type **6.95**, then tap RETURN.

Tap TAB, type **Tulips**.

Tap TAB, type **3.98**, then tap RETURN.

8 *Close document without saving changes.*

Use tab leaders

When you use a tab stop, you can easily put a row of dots, dashes, or underlines in the space before the tab stop.

1 **Open new document (unless you just started Word).**

2 **Create single tab stop with leader:**

On **Format** menu, choose **Tabs**.

Duplicate this **Tabs** dialog box:

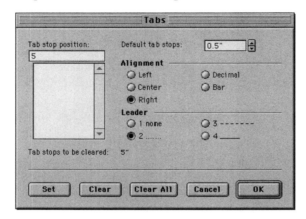

It sets one right tab stop with dotted leader extending from text to 5" mark on ruler.

Click **OK**.

3 **Enter two lines using new tab stop:**

Type **Chapter 1**. Tap TAB. Type **1**. Tap RETURN.

Type **Chapter 2**. Tap TAB. Type **12**. Tap RETURN.

4 **Use different types of tab leaders:**

On **Format** menu, choose **Tabs**.

Tabs dialog box opens. Tab at 5 inches should be selected. If not, click to select.

Under **Leader**, choose **3** (dashed line).

Click **OK**.

For chapters 3 and 4, use dashed-line leader shown below.

For chapters 5 and 6, use solid-line leader shown below.

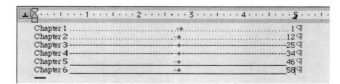

5 **Close document without saving changes.**

STOP *Letter as completed on page 13 must be on floppy disk.*

Define paragraph styles

You can give a name to any combination of paragraph and character formats. Then you can apply the formats by name. **DOC / 39**

1 **Open Letter document.**

2 **View current styles in document:**

At left end of formatting toolbar, click or press ▪ at right of word **Normal** to see style list.

Every new document you create comes with these named styles.

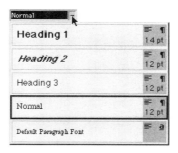

Border is around Normal. *This is style of paragraph with insertion point.*

Click or drag back to ▪ again to close style list.

3 **Apply named style to selected paragraph:**

Click anywhere in paragraph 2.

On style list, choose **Heading 1**.

Notice changes in text. Whole paragraph is affected.

Click anywhere in paragraph 3.

On style list, choose **Heading 2**.

4 **Remove applied styles:**

With (SHIFT) held down, click anywhere in paragraph 2.

Some text should be highlighted in paragraphs 2 and 3.

On style list, choose **Normal**.

Both paragraphs return to original formatting.

5 **Prepare custom paragraph style:**

Click anywhere in paragraph 1.

On **Format** menu, choose **Paragraph**.

In **Indentation** area, set **Left** and **Right** to 1 inch.

On **Special** list, choose **First line**. Leave 0.5" in **By** text box.

On **Line spacing** list, choose **1.5 lines**.

Click **OK** to see result.

Paragraph 1 should have all formats you just defined for it.

Tip

Using named styles for all paragraphs in a document has two benefits. First, it makes headings and body paragraphs consistent throughout the document. Second, if you change the definition of a style, all paragraphs with that named style are automatically updated.

6 *Create new style based on paragraph formatting:*

Click ▢ (style name) to highlight **Normal**.

Type **indented** and tap ⟨RETURN⟩.

> *Style named "indented" is created.*

Watch style name on formatting toolbar as you click in each paragraph.

> *Paragraph 1 has indented style; rest have Normal style.*

7 *Apply new paragraph style:*

Click anywhere in paragraph 3.

On style list, choose **indented**.

> *Paragraph 3 changes to indented style.*

8 *Change formats in paragraph 1:*

Highlight any characters in paragraph 1.

> *You'll add some character formats now.*

On **Format** menu, choose **Font**.

On **Font** list, choose **Arial**.

On **Font style** list, choose **Italic**.

On **Size** list, choose **12**.

Click **OK**.

> *So far, changes have affected only highlighted text in paragraph 1.*

9 *Add new character formats to definition of indented style:*

Make sure same characters are still highlighted.

On style list, choose **indented**.

> *Modify Style dialog box gives you two choices. You want first.*

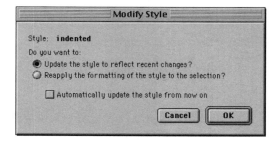

With first choice selected, click **OK**.

> *All characters in both indented paragraphs now have new style.*

10 *Close document without saving changes.*

By the way
You can also create character styles. Format sample text using the desired styles, then select it. On the Format menu, choose Style; click New and designate Character as the style type. The character style also appears on the style menu.

Add graphic object

You can add a graphic to a word processing document.
Microsoft Word contains a gallery of clip art you can use.

1 **Open Opening document.**

2 **Insert graphic:**

Click to place insertion point to left of *P* in title **Petal Pushers Flower Shop**.

On **Insert** menu, choose **Picture**; on submenu, choose **Clip Art**.

In **Category** list, click **Plants**.

Click **Love Flower** (or other image if missing).

> **No clip art files?**
>
> *If you did not do a complete installation of Microsoft Office, the clip art files may be missing. If so, click Cancel and quit Microsoft Word. You'll need the original Office CD or disks. The clip art folder is in the Microsoft Office 98 folder. Drag it to the desired location on your computer.*

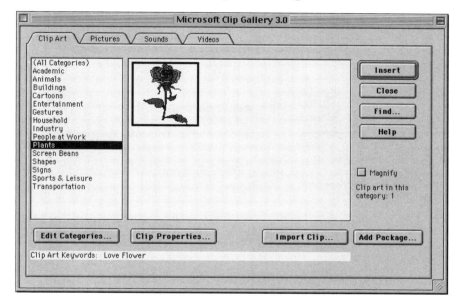

Click **Insert**.

> *Picture is inserted next to title. Word now appears in Page Layout view. Graphic images do not appear in Normal view. Picture palette appears.*

3 **Adjust size of graphic:**

On picture palette, click 🖼 (format picture button).

In dialog box, click **Size** tab.

In **Scale** section, change **Height** to **25%**. Note that Width changes too.

> **No picture palette?**
>
> *The picture palette should automatically appear when the graphic is selected. If not, on the View menu, choose Toolbars, then from the submenu, choose Picture.*

Click **OK**.

4 **Switch to Normal view:**

On **View** menu, choose **Normal**.

> *Graphic does not appear in Normal view.*

5 **Save document with new graphic.**

Copy between documents

You can easily transfer text from one document to another using the computer's clipboard.

1 *Copy text:*

Highlight all text in **Opening** document.

On **Edit** menu, choose **Copy** (or click 🖺 on standard toolbar).

2 *Open document to receive text:*

Open **Letter**.

Insertion point is at beginning of document.

> *This is where text will be inserted.*

3 *Insert copied text and graphic:*

On **Edit** menu, choose **Paste** (or click 🖺 on standard toolbar).

4 *Adjust placement:*

Tap [RETURN] to move original text down.

Tip

To see graphic, on View *menu, choose* Page Layout.

5 *Paste copied text and graphic into new document:*

On standard toolbar, click ▯ (new tool).

On **Edit** menu, choose **Paste** (or click 🖺 on standard toolbar).

> *Same text and graphic are pasted. Copied text remains on clipboard until replaced or computer is shut down.*

6 *Repeat paste in new document:*

Tap [RETURN] twice to skip lines, then, on **Edit** menu, choose **Paste** (or click 🖺 on standard toolbar).

7 *View graphic in new document:*

On **View** menu, choose **Page Layout**.

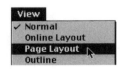

> *Graphic appears in both pasted copies!*

8 *Close all documents:*

Press and hold [SHIFT] down. On **File** menu, choose **Close All**. Do *not* save changes in any documents.

Use AutoText entries

Microsoft Word has built-in text entries you can use to speed up document creation. You can also create your own entries.

1 Create new document using ▢ (new tool).

2 View AutoText palette:

On **Insert** menu, choose **AutoText**.

On submenu, choose **Closing**.

Submenu of closing entries appears.

Choose one you like.

Text is inserted in document.

3 Insert other entries using method in step 2.

4 Create custom AutoText entry:

Tap RETURN to move to blank line in document.

Type **Petal Pushers Flower Shop**.

Format text as **14 point, bold**.

Select text.

(To include formatting in AutoText entry, be sure to also select ¶ at end.)

On **Insert** menu, choose **AutoText**.

On submenu, choose **New**.

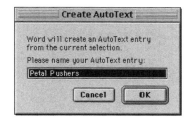

Click **OK** to accept suggested name.

5 Insert custom AutoText in document:

Tap RETURN to move to blank line in document.

Type **Peta**. Note information box that appears above typing.

Tap RETURN to insert suggested AutoText entry.

Entry is inserted.

6 Close document without saving changes.

Insert page breaks

Microsoft Word automatically starts a new page when necessary. You can also add manual page breaks.

1 **Create two-page document:**

Open **Letter**. If necessary, on **View** menu, choose **Normal**.

Highlight text from top down through blank line before *Sincerely*.

On **Edit** menu, choose **Copy** (or tap ⌘C).

Tap ⌘HOME to move insertion point to beginning of document.

On **Edit** menu, choose **Paste** (or tap ⌘V).

Repeat last step six or seven times.

2 **Save for future use:**

On **File** menu, choose **Save As**. Save with name **Two Pages** on floppy disk.

3 **View automatic page break:**

Using scroll bar, move through document until you see dotted line across page.

Dotted line shows where new page begins when document is printed.

4 **Select location for manual page break:**

Click to put insertion point anywhere in text a few lines above dotted line.

5 **Insert page break (method 1):**

On **Insert** menu, choose **Break**.

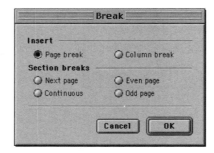

If necessary, click to select **Page break**, then click **OK**.

Manual break appears as dense dotted line with words Page Break. *Note that automatic page break has disappeared.*

By the way
The page break line stands for the nonprinting page break character. As with any other character, you can highlight it, copy it, paste it, and delete it.

6 **Remove page break:**

Click to left of **Page Break** line to highlight it. Tap DELETE.

7 **Insert page break (method 2):**

Tap SHIFT ENTER (*not* SHIFT RETURN; ENTER is at far right of keyboard on numeric keypad).

Page break is inserted.

Complete previous activity before going on.

Preview document

It is always a good idea to preview a document to see page breaks before printing.

1 **Preview both pages of document:**

On **File** menu, choose **Print Preview**.

Preview toolbar replaces others. Page appears at reduced scale.

Press and drag ▦ (multiple pages tool) on preview toolbar to see two side-by-side pages (see figure at left).

2 **Zoom in (method 1):**

Position pointer over page you want to view more closely.

If pointer has arrow shape, click mouse button to select page.

Pointer changes shape to ⊕ *(magnifying glass with plus sign).*

Click magnifying-glass pointer at area you want to zoom in on.

Percentage view is increased, and location where you clicked appears.

3 **Zoom out (method 1):**

Position pointer over enlarged page.

Pointer now has minus sign ⊖ *.*

Click page to zoom out.

4 **Zoom in (method 2):**

Click or press ▾ on preview toolbar to see zoom-percent list.

Select **100%**.

View percentage increases.

5 **Zoom out (method 2):**

View zoom list again.

Click to select **Two Pages**.

View percentage decreases. Two pages appear again.

6 **Explore other buttons on toolbar:**

Notice ▤ (print tool) on preview toolbar.

You could print document now. Instead, you'll exit preview.

7 **Exit preview:**

Click `Close` on preview toolbar to return to normal view.

8 **Close document without saving changes.**

Two Pages document must be on floppy disk. See page 44.

46 / *Word Processing with Microsoft Word*

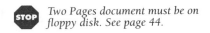

Change page margins

You can set all four margins on the page. Paragraph indents automatically adjust to the new margins.

1 Open Two Pages document.

2 View margin controls:

On **Format** menu, choose **Document**.

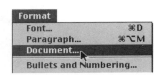

If necessary, click **Margins** tab to bring page of dialog box into view.

> *Top four numbers at left are sizes of page margins now.*

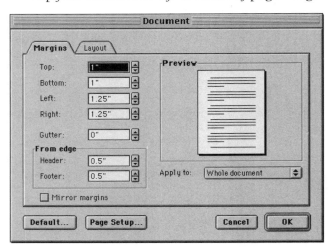

3 Change margins and see results:

Change left margin to 3 inches and right margin to 1 inch. Click **OK**.

On **File** menu, choose **Print Preview** to see effect.

Click Close on preview toolbar when you're ready to go on.

4 Mirror even and odd pages:

On **Format** menu, choose **Document**.

Watch **Left** and **Right** labels and **Preview** area as you click **Mirror margins** check box at lower left.

> *Labels change to* Inside *and* Outside. *Mirrored pages are for documents that will be printed on both sides and need extra inside space for binding.*

5 Look at other options:

Note options in **From edge** area.

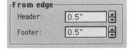

> *Numbers here control distance of headers and footers from top and bottom of paper. (You'll learn about headers and footers on page 48.)*

Note **Apply to** list box.

> *Margin changes can apply to whole document or from this point on.*

6 Cancel dialog box and close document without saving changes.

Add columns & column breaks

Microsoft Word allows you to put more than one column of text on each page. You can also adjust where columns break.

1 Open Two Pages document.

2 Create two-column layout for whole document:

On **Format** menu, choose **Columns**.

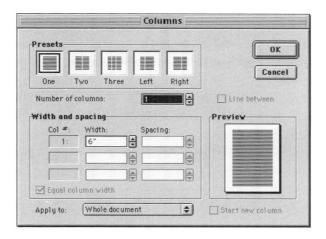

In **Presets** area, click icon labeled **Two**. Click **OK**.

You see changes immediately in page layout view.

3 Preview to see entire document:

On **File** menu, choose **Print Preview**.

Document appears in two columns with automatic column break.

Click Close on preview toolbar.

4 On View menu, choose Normal to return to normal view.

5 Insert manual column break:

Tap ⌘ HOME to go to beginning of document.

Click at beginning of fourth paragraph.

On **Insert** menu, choose **Break**, then choose **Column Break**. Click **OK**.

6 Preview document again. Note that column breaks at place you chose.

7 Return document to single column:

Do not exit preview. You can adjust formatting in this view.

On **Format** menu, choose **Columns**.

Under **Presets**, click icon labeled **One**, then click **OK**.

Note that column break now serves as page break.

8 Close document without saving changes.

STOP *Two Pages document must be on floppy disk. See page 44.*

48 / *Word Processing with Microsoft Word*

Add headers & footers

A header or footer can be used to put titles and page numbers at the top or bottom of each page.

1 **Open Two Pages document.**

2 **Go to header and footer view:**

On **View** menu, choose **Header and Footer**.

> *Page shows dashed outline for header area.*

In **Header and Footer** palette, move pointer to each tool icon and read its description. *Don't click tools yet!*

3 **Enter header text:**

Note insertion point in header area of page. Look at tab stop in ruler:

> *Ruler shows center tab stop at 3" mark and right tab stop at 6" mark.*

Tap ⌜TAB⌟ twice to move insertion point to right tab stop at 6" mark.

Type **Petal Pushers**.

4 **Move to footer area:**

On **Header and Footer** palette, click 🔲 (switch between header and footer).

> *Command brings footer area in view and puts insertion point there. Ruler settings are same as for header.*

5 **Enter footer text:**

Note center tab stop at 3" mark.

On **Header and Footer** palette, click **Insert AutoText**.

On list, choose **-PAGE-**.

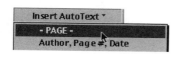

> *You should see –1– in middle of footer area.*

In text window, tap ⌜TAB⌟ to move to right tab stop at 6" mark.

On **Header and Footer** palette, click 🔲 (insert date button).

> *Current date is inserted. (Date is updated when you open or print document.)*

6 **Close view of header and footer:**

On **Header and Footer** palette, click ⌜Close⌟.

7 **Preview header and footer:**

On **File** menu, choose **Print Preview**.

Zoom in to see header and footer.

8 *Make headers and footers different on first page:*

Often, you want different headers and footers, or none at all, on first page.

On **Format** menu, choose **Document**.

Click **Layout** tab.

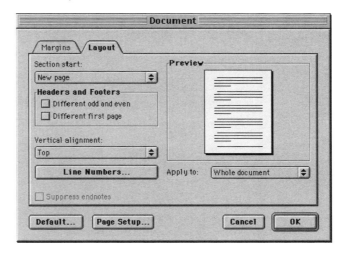

In **Headers and Footers** area, click to place mark in **Different first page** check box.

Click **OK**.

9 *View results in Print Preview, then click* Close *to exit preview.*

10 *Add special header on page 1:*

Tap ⌘ HOME to move insertion point to beginning of document.

On **View** menu, choose **Header and Footer**.

New header is first page header.

With insertion point in header area, tap TAB and type **Flowers**.

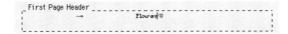

11 *View results:*

On **File** menu, choose **Print Preview**.

Click to magnify view of each page and see header.

Header on first page is different.

Click Close to exit preview.

12 *Close document without saving changes.*

STOP *Two Pages document must be on floppy disk. See page 44.*

Create & modify sections

Sections are like chapters in a book. Each section can have different header, page margins, and number of columns.

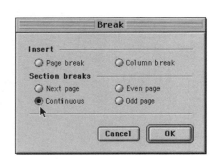

1 *Open Two Pages document.*

2 *Add section break before paragraph 4:*

Put insertion point just before first word in paragraph 4.

On **Insert** menu, choose **Break**.

Look at four options in **Section breaks** area.

All but Continuous *will cause next section to begin new page.*

In **Section breaks** area, choose **Continuous**. Click **OK**.

Nonprinting section break character is inserted. Symbol for character is double row of dotted lines with Section Break (Continuous) *in middle.*

3 *Preview document:*

On **File** menu, choose **Print Preview**.

So far, you see no change. Both sections have same format.

Click Close to exit preview.

4 *Change format of section 2:*

Click anywhere below **Section Break** line.

On **Format** menu, choose **Columns**.

Under **Presets**, click icon labeled **Three**.

Click **OK**.

Document appears in page layout view. First three paragraphs are in single column. Rest are in three columns.

> **Tip**
> *The format change affects just the section with the insertion point (or selected text).*

5 *Preview entire document and see results:*

On **File** menu, choose **Print Preview**.

When finished, click Close to exit preview.

6 *Return to normal view:*

On **View** menu, choose **Normal**.

7 *Delete section break and see result:*

Click at left of **Section Break** line to highlight it.

Tap DELETE.

On **File** menu, choose **Print Preview**. Click Close when finished.

Note that entire document is now in three-column format.

8 *Close document without saving changes.*

STOP *Letter as completed on page 13 must be on floppy disk.*

Create & format tables

You can easily add tabular information to a Microsoft Word document without setting tab stops.

1 **Open Letter.**

2 **Prepare to insert table after paragraph 1:**

Click just right of paragraph mark at end of paragraph 1.

Tap [RETURN] twice.

> *Insertion point should be in middle blank line. You'll insert table here. It's always good to leave blank space around table.*

3 **Insert table:**

On **Table** menu, choose **Insert Table**.

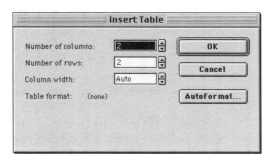

Type **4** for **Number of columns**; tap [TAB]; type **4** for **Number of rows**. Click **OK**.

> *Empty table with four columns and four rows appears in document. Rectangles formed by intersections of rows and columns are called "cells."*

4 **Enter data in table:**

> *Insertion point should already be in first cell.*

Tap [TAB] to move to next cell. (First one stays blank.)

Type **January**, then tap [TAB] to move to next cell.

Type **February**, then tap [TAB] to move to next cell.

Type **March**, then tap [TAB] to move to next cell.

> *Insertion point moves to next row.*

Type **Tulip**, then tap [TAB] to move to next cell.

Continue entering text to create table shown below:

	January	February	March	
Tulip	19	18	15	
Rose	39	34	36	
Daisy	15	19	25	

5 **Save document with new name:**

On **File** menu, choose **Save As**. Save with name **Table** on floppy disk.

Tip

If AutoText entries for the months appear, tap [RETURN] to accept them. You can learn more about AutoText entries on page 43.

6 *Select rows and columns and entire table:*

Put arrow pointer just left of row 2. Click to select whole row.

Put pointer just above column 3. Watch pointer change to ⬇. Click to select column.

With (OPTION) held down, click anywhere in column 2 to select it.

With (OPTION) held down, double-click anywhere in table to select all cells.

7 *Format table:*

Select row 1.

On formatting toolbar, click 🅱 (bold tool) to add bold to months.

Select column 1.

On formatting toolbar, click 🅱 twice to add bold to flower names.

8 *Adjust column width:*

Select all cells in table.

With (SHIFT) held down, on ruler, put pointer over first column divider (at 1.5 inches). Watch pointer change to small double-ended arrow and information box appear.

Press and drag left to 1" mark.

> *Width of column 1 is reduced to 1 inch.*

Use above steps to adjust other column widths to 1 inch also.

	January	February	March	
Tulip	19	18	15	
Rose	39	34	36	
Daisy	15	19	25	

9 *Select columns 2, 3, and 4.*

Position pointer at top of column 2.

Watch for pointer to change to ⬇.

Press and drag to right, being careful to keep pointer in table.

10 *Change text alignment:*

On formatting toolbar, click ☰ (center alignment tool).

> *Text is centered within cells in all three columns.*

11 *Center table on page:*

Select all cells in table.

On **Table** menu, choose **Cell Height and Width**.

> *Dialog box like figure on next page appears.*

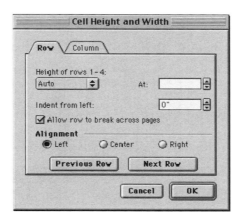

In **Alignment** area, choose **Center**, then click **OK**.

Table is centered on page.

12 *Add shading:*

Select all cells in row 1.

On **Format** menu, choose **Borders and Shading**.

Click **Shading** tab.

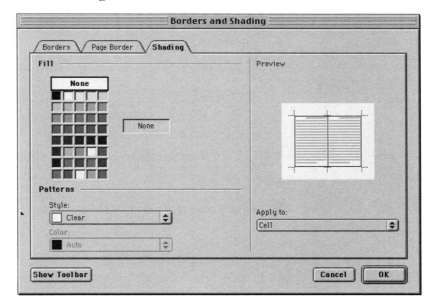

In **Fill** area, choose shade of gray in middle of second row.

Click **OK**.

Click outside table to observe formatting.

	January	February	March
Tulip	19	18	15
Rose	39	34	36
Daisy	15	19	25

13 *Save changed document.*

14 *Close document.*

STOP *Letter as completed on page 13 must be on floppy disk.*

Use mail merge

You can create a form letter and a data document with names and addresses. Then you can merge the two.

1 **Open new document for name and address data:**

On standard toolbar, click ⬜ (new tool).

> *Mail merge data document is ordinary word processor document with table containing data you want used. Next step is to insert blank table.*

2 **Insert table to hold data:**

On **Table** menu, choose **Insert Table**.

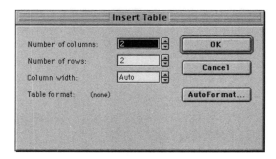

Type **6** for **Number of columns**; tap TAB; type **4** for **Number of rows**. Click **OK**.

> *Six columns will hold first name, last name, address, city, state, zip code.*

3 **Enter headings in first row:**

> *Insertion point should already be in first cell.*

Type following text:

> **First** TAB **Last** TAB **Address** TAB **City** TAB
> **State** TAB **Zipcode**

> *Column headings are names of data fields. You'll use these field names in your form letter instead of any actual data for a person.*

4 **Enter name and address data:**

Tap TAB to go to first cell in next row.

Enter data shown in figure below, tapping TAB between entries. Substitute your own name and address in first row.

> *Don't worry if text wraps to next line. It won't affect mail merge.*

First¤	Last¤	Address¤	City¤	State¤	Zipcode¤	¤
Bonita¤	Sebastian¤	3045 John Muir¤	San Francisco¤	CA¤	94132¤	¤
Diego¤	Rivera¤	137 Alamo¤	San Antonio¤	TX¤	78213¤	¤
Jasper¤	Johns¤	301 Broadway¤	New York¤	NY¤	10019¤	¤

5 **Save and close data document:**

On **File** menu, choose **Save As**. Save with name **People** on floppy disk.

On **File** menu, choose **Close**.

6 *Open, rename, and save document to become form:*

Open **Letter** from your floppy disk.

> *Form document will be letter based on this.*

On **File** menu, choose **Save As**. Save with name **Form Letter** on floppy disk.

7 *Convert document to form for mail merge:*

On **Tools** menu, choose **Mail Merge**.

> *You'll use this dialog box to create form (main document, step 1), link it to data document (step 2), and merge both (step 3).*

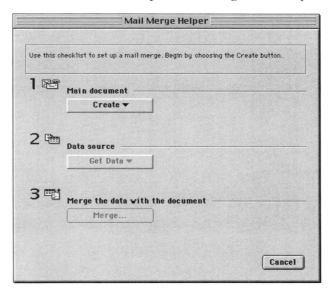

Click **Create** button.

On **Create** list, choose **Form Letters**.

> *Following message box appears:*

Click **Active Window**.

> Form Letter *is now set as main document for mail merge. (To convert form back to normal Word document, you would use last option on* Create *list.)*

By the way
You can use the same data document to print mailing labels or to print envelopes. The starting point is the Create *list above. Then click the* New Main Document *button to create the form document that matches your labels or envelopes.*

8 *Link form document to data document:*

In **Data source** section in **Mail Merge Helper**, click **Get Data** button.

On **Get Data** list, choose **Open Data Source**.

Open **People** from your floppy disk.

In message box saying you have no merge fields in document, click **Edit Main Document**.

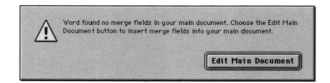

9 *Insert fields from data document into form document:*

View merge helper toolbar below other toolbars.

Make sure insertion point is at beginning of document.

Click **Insert Merge Field** to see list. Choose **First**.

 «First» *is inserted into form document at insertion point.*

Tap (SPACEBAR) to insert space character.

On **Insert Merge Field** list, choose **Last**.

 «Last» *is inserted.*

Tap (RETURN) to move down a line.

On **Insert Merge Field** list, choose **Address**. Tap (RETURN).

On **Insert Merge Field** list, choose **City**.

Type a comma and one space.

On **Insert Merge Field** list, choose **State**. Tap (SPACEBAR) twice.

On **Insert Merge Field** list, choose **Zipcode**. Tap (RETURN) twice.

Type **Dear** and one space.

On **Insert Merge Field** list, choose **First**.

Type a comma and tap (RETURN) twice.

 Beginning of document should look like figure at left.

If Office Assistant appears, click **Cancel**.

10 *Save Form Letter document.*

11 *Perform mail merge (with error checking):*

On merge helper toolbar, click 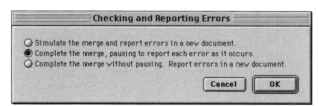 (check for errors tool).

Click **OK**.

> *Single mail merge document named* Form Letters1 *is created; errors, if any, appear. (If there are errors, take care of them and perform mail merge again.)*

12 *Review letters:*

Scroll through new **Form Letters1** document and look at inside addresses.

> *Letters are separated by section breaks (ones that also start new pages).*

13 *Preview merged letters:*

On **File** menu, choose **Print Preview**.

Use ▦ (multiple pages tool) to see all pages.

Zoom in to see inside address on each page.

Click **Close** when finished.

14 *Save merged document:*

On **File** menu, choose **Save** (or **Save As**).

Save file with name **Merge** on floppy disk.

15 *Print merged letters (optional):*

On **File** menu, choose **Print**. Click **OK** button.

16 *Close all documents:*

Press and hold (SHIFT) down.

On **File** menu, choose **Close All**.

If asked, save changes.

17 *Quit Microsoft Word:*

On **File** menu, choose **Quit**.

Create Web page document

Microsoft Word allows you to create a "World-Wide Web" page.
Using Word and the Web Page wizard makes this task easy!

1 *Start Microsoft Word.*

2 *Open Web Page wizard:*

On **File** menu, choose **New**. (Do *not* click ⬚ on standard toolbar.)

In dialog box, click **Web Pages** tab.

Click **Web Page Wizard**, then click **OK**.

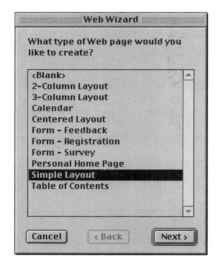

Web Page Wizard

3 *Choose type of Web page:*

> **No Web Page menus?**
> *You may need to increase the amount of memory that is allocated to Word. Quit Word, then click the Word application icon. On the File menu, choose Get Info, then increase the memory in the Preferred text box. Close the window, then re-open Word.*

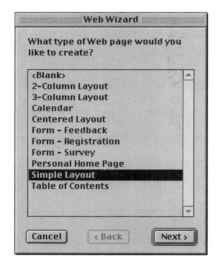

With **Simple Layout** selected, click **Next**.

4 *Choose design of Web page:*

Click **Contemporary**, then click **Finish**.

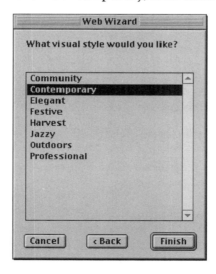

> **Important!**
> *Be sure that HTML Document is selected in file type list.*

5 *Save Web page document:*

On **File** menu, choose **Save**. Save with name **Web Page** on floppy disk.

6 *Enter and format text:*

Select text placeholders and enter replacement text to create document shown below.

Make text bold. Increase font size as in figure (use **A A** for changes).

7 *Add graphic to page:*

Click just to right of *s* in *providers.*

   Location is where graphic will be anchored.

On standard toolbar, click 🖼 (insert picture button).

In dialog box, locate Microsoft Office 98 Clip Art folder.

In **Popular** folder, choose **Flower**. Click **Insert**.

8 *Resize graphic image:*

Click graphic.

Carefully position pointer over small black handle in lower-right corner.

Press and drag up and to left to reduce size.

9 *Wrap text around graphic:*

Click graphic.

On **Picture** palette, click ▣ (left wrapping button).

   Text wraps around graphic.

10 *Save and close Web Page document.*

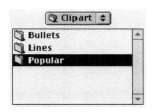

By the way
If a green zig zag line appears under Your, *it means the grammar checker is calling your attention to a possible problem.*

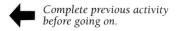
Convert document & view HTML

You can convert an existing document to a Web page document. Word creates the hypertext markup language.

1 Open and edit Promo document:

On **File** menu, choose **Open**, then select **Promo** document on floppy disk.

Delete paragraph 3, letter closing, and **P.S.** (letters only).

2 Save document as Web page document:

On **File** menu, choose **Save as HTML** (hypertext markup language).

Save on floppy with name **Promo Web**.

Click **Save**.

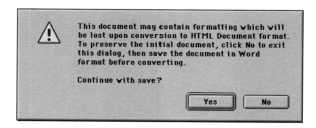

Click **Yes** to continue save.

Close saved document.

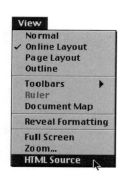

3 Open and view Web page document:

On **File** menu, choose **Web Page** in documents section at bottom.

On **View** menu, choose **HTML Source**.

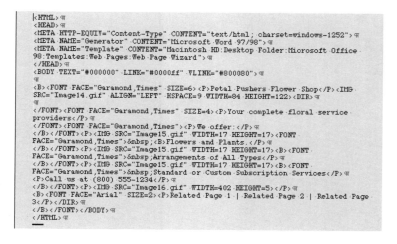

4 Hide code:

On standard toolbar, click Exit HTML Source.

← *Complete previous activity before going on.*

Create link to another page

You can create a link in one Web page that when clicked, takes the user to another page.

1 **Insert Hyperlink to Promo Web document:**

Select text, **Related Page 1**.

Type **Promotion**.

> *Original text is replaced.*

Select text again and on **Insert** menu, choose **Hyperlink**.

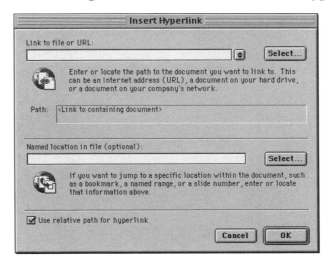

In **Link to file or URL** area, click **Select** button.

Locate and open **Promo Web** document.

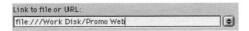

Document name appears in **Link to file or URL** list.

Click **OK**.

2 **Try link:**

Position pointer over **Promotion**. Note pointer shape.

Tap mouse button.

> *Promo Web document appears.*

3 **Return to Web Page document and save change:**

On **Go** menu on Web toolbar, choose **Back**.

On **File** menu, choose **Save**.

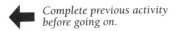 *Complete previous activity before going on.*

View page in Web browser & edit HTML

You can open your Web page using the browser you use to access the Internet. You can make changes by editing the HTML.

File
New...
Open...   ⌘O
Open Web Page...
Close   ⌘W
Save   ⌘S
Save As...
Save as Word Document...
Web Page Preview...
Page Setup...

By the way
If you do not have a Web page browser installed on your computer, you will not be able to see this view; however, you have already seen a close facsimile in the Word HTML document.

Tip
For information on uploading a Web page to the Internet, contact your Internet service provider.

1 *View page in Web browser:*

On **File** menu, choose **Web Page Preview**.

Page appears in Internet Explorer or Netscape.

2 *Close Web browser:*

On **File** menu, choose **Close**.

3 *Edit HTML text:*

If necessary, open **Web Page** document in Microsoft Word.

On **View** menu, choose **HTML Source**.

Locate code for related pages.

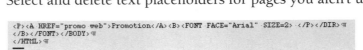

Select and delete text placeholders for pages you aren't using.

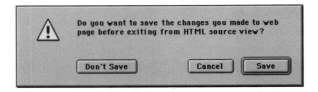

On **View** menu, choose **Exit HTML Source**.

View
✓ Normal
  Online Layout
  Page Layout
✓ Ruler
  Reveal Formatting
  Full Screen
  Zoom...
  Exit HTML Source

Click **Save** to save changes.

4 *View edited Web Page document in browser.*

5 *Close all files and quit Microsoft Word.*

Start Microsoft PowerPoint

You are now ready to start the Microsoft PowerPoint application running on your computer.

By the way
You won't be creating a presentation now. Instead, from here through page 82, you'll be learning how to use drawing tools to create graphic objects. After that, you'll be able to use the same tools to create and modify slides in presentations.
The drawing tools you learn here are also available in Word and Excel for adding graphics in those applications.

1 **Start computer and PowerPoint:**

Switch on computer (see page 2).

Start Microsoft PowerPoint (see page 7, but choose Microsoft PowerPoint this time).

If **Office Assistant** appears, click **Start using Microsoft PowerPoint**. Then close **Office Assistant** window.

2 **Note options on PowerPoint dialog box:**

PowerPoint *dialog box is starting point for creating new presentation or opening existing one.*

By the way
You can only reach this dialog box when you first start the PowerPoint application.

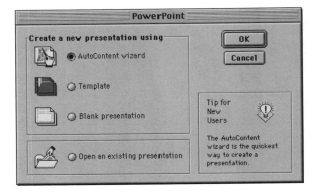

3 **Use help balloons to explore options:**

On **Help** menu, choose **Show Balloons**.

Position pointer over **AutoContent Wizard**. Do *not* press mouse button.

Read description of option.

By the way
With System 7.6 or earlier, the help menu is the question-mark icon near the right end of the menu bar.

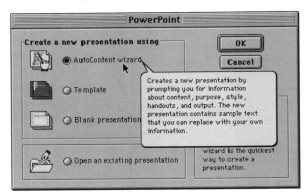

Tip
Whenever you see a new dialog box, feel free to use the help balloons to find out about all the options. Then continue with the steps in the book.

Repeat above steps for other three options.

Wizard and template options are shortcuts for making complete presentations You'll start with blank presentation to work with graphics.

On **Help** menu, choose **Hide Balloons**.

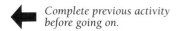 *Complete previous activity before going on.*

Create new document

You will create a new blank document with a blank page for learning to use the drawing tools in Microsoft PowerPoint.

1 **Create new blank document:**

In **Create a new presentation using** area of dialog box, choose **Blank presentation**.

Click **OK**.

2 **Create blank layout:**

Tip
Think of a slide as a page in a word processing document.

In **New Slide** dialog box, use vertical scroll bar to see layout icons.

Click icon for **Blank** layout. Click **OK**.

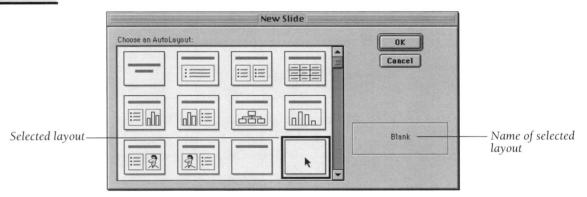

Selected layout ——

—— Name of selected layout

3 **View Microsoft PowerPoint screen with blank layout:**

Menu bar ——
Standard toolbar ——
Formatting toolbar ——
Title bar ——

Area for drawing ——

View scale (yours may be different)

Common Tasks palette

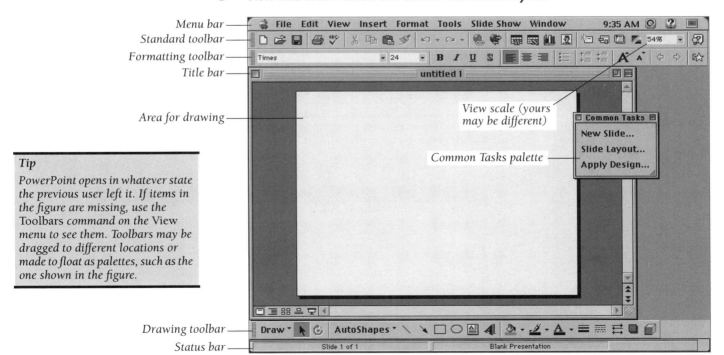

Tip
PowerPoint opens in whatever state the previous user left it. If items in the figure are missing, use the Toolbars command on the View menu to see them. Toolbars may be dragged to different locations or made to float as palettes, such as the one shown in the figure.

Drawing toolbar ——
Status bar ——

4 **Explore drawing tools:**

Put pointer on each word and icon on drawing toolbar. Read description.

Toolbar has tools and menus for creating and formatting graphical objects.

Save file

After creating a new document, you should name it and save it permanently on disk.

1 *Insert floppy disk:*

Insert disk, slider end first with label side up, into floppy drive.

2 *Give Save command:*

On **File** menu, choose **Save** (or click 🖫 on standard toolbar, or tap ⌘ S).

3 *Name presentation document:*

Note blinking insertion point in **Save** text box at bottom.

Type **Drawing**.

4 *Say where to save document:*

Click [**Desktop**] (desktop button) at right of dialog box.

Double-click 🖫 **Work Disk** (floppy disk icon) on list in center of dialog box.

Save dialog box should look like figure below.

Location where you want document saved

Name of document

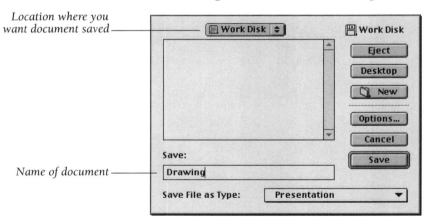

Click **Save** to save document with name **Drawing** on floppy disk.

Title bar now shows new file name.

Draw graphic objects

Microsoft Office provides tools to add simple or complex graphics that you draw to a slide or entire presentation.

1 **Look at drawing tools:**

If **Common Tasks** palette is in view, click its close box.

> *You won't be using this palette. Same commands are on menus.*

If drawing toolbar is hidden, choose **Toolbars** on **View** menu, then **Drawing** on submenu.

> *Toolbar normally appears at bottom of screen.*

Move pointer to drawing toolbar. For each tool, read name below pointer.

2 **Draw simple object:**

On drawing toolbar, click ☐ (rectangle tool).

Release mouse button.

> *Light gray highlight shows which tool is active.*

Position pointer near upper-left corner of slide area.

> *Pointer shape is now crosshair.*

Press mouse button and drag diagonally down and to right.

Release mouse button.

> *Colored rectangle with black outline appears where you drew. Highlight goes to ▶ (selection tool) at left of drawing toolbar. Pointer shape is arrow now.*

3 **Deselect and select object:**

Note handles (tiny white squares) on border of object.

> *Handles show object is selected.*

Click arrow pointer in clear area of slide to deselect rectangle.

> *Handles disappear.*

Click arrow pointer inside rectangle.

Note handles.

> *Object is selected again.*

Move, resize & delete object

After you have created an object, you may wish to modify it by moving it, changing its size or shape, or deleting it.

1 *Move object (method 1):*

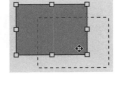

Point inside rectangle. Note change in pointer shape.

Press mouse button and drag to right.

Release mouse button.

Rectangle moves to new location.

2 *Move object (method 2):*

If object has no handles, click inside object to select it.

Watch object as you tap each arrow key on keyboard three or four times.

Object moves in small increments in direction of arrow.

3 *Make object smaller:*

If object has no handles, click inside object to select it.

Move pointer carefully to handle at lower right.

Note change in pointer shape.

Press mouse button and drag handle up and to left.

Release mouse button.

Rectangle is smaller.

4 *Make object larger:*

Follow above steps except drag handle down and to right.

Release mouse button.

Rectangle is larger.

5 *Change shape of object:*

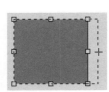

If object has no handles, click inside object to select it.

Move pointer carefully to handle at middle of right side.

Note change in pointer shape.

Press mouse button and drag handle to right.

Release mouse button.

Rectangle is wider.

6 *Delete object:*

If object has no handles, click inside object to select it.

Tap (DELETE).

Use drawing aids

*Freehand drawing can be difficult. Microsoft PowerPoint has
aids to ease the task.*

1 *Draw equal-sided object:*

On drawing toolbar, click ▣ (rectangle tool). Release mouse button.

On keyboard, hold (SHIFT) down.

Position pointer near upper-left corner of slide area.

Press mouse button and drag down and to right.

Release mouse button first, then release (SHIFT).

> *Equal-sided rectangle (square) appears.*

2 *Move object horizontally or vertically:*

If object has no handles, click inside object to select it.

On keyboard, hold (SHIFT) down.

Try to press and drag to right and down.

> *You can move object only horizontally or vertically while pressing (SHIFT).*

3 *Resize object without changing shape:*

If object has no handles, click inside object to select it.

On keyboard, hold (SHIFT) down.

Move pointer over handle at lower right.

Press and drag to right and down.

> *Object is enlarged but keeps shape.*

4 *Delete object:*

If object has no handles, click inside object to select it.

Tap (DELETE).

5 *Draw object from center out:*

On drawing toolbar, click ◯ (oval tool). Release mouse button.

On keyboard, press and hold (OPTION).

Position pointer near middle of slide area.

Press mouse button and drag down and to right.

> *Oval grows in all directions from place where you began to drag.*

Release mouse button first, then release (OPTION).

6 *Delete object:*

If oval has no handles, click inside object to select it.

Tap (DELETE).

7 *Draw equal-sided object from center out:*

On drawing toolbar, click ▣ (rectangle tool). Release mouse button.

On keyboard, hold both (OPTION) and (SHIFT) down.

From middle of slide area, drag down and to right. Release button and keys.

Square is drawn from center out.

8 *Use guides:*

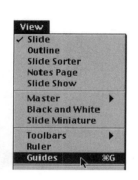

On **View** menu, choose **Guides**.

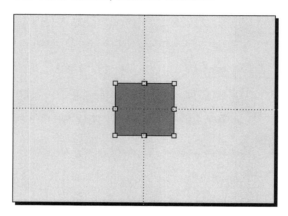

Dotted horizontal and vertical guides appear.

Put pointer on vertical guide (outside square). Press and drag to right.

Note that distance (in inches from center) appears at pointer.

Watch square as you drag it near either guide.

Edge or center of square "jumps" to guide.

Delete square.

9 *Use guides to position new object:*

On drawing toolbar, click ◯ (oval tool). Release mouse button.

On keyboard, press and hold (OPTION)(SHIFT).

Position pointer near intersection of guides.

Press mouse button and drag down and to right.

Result is perfect circle with center exactly at place guides cross.

Delete circle.

10 *Switch guides off:*

On **View** menu, choose **Guides** again.

11 *Close file without saving changes.*

Drawing file must be on floppy disk. See page 65.

Draw more objects

The drawing toolbar has other tools for creating objects. They work like the rectangle tool. You will explore them now.

1 ***Open Drawing file.***

Make sure you see blank slide. If necessary, delete any objects on slide.

2 ***Use steps below to draw objects in this figure:***

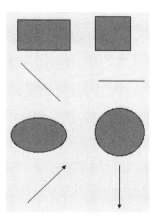

3 ***Draw objects shown at left side of figure:***

To draw object, first click proper tool. After releasing mouse button, move crosshair pointer to one corner where you intend to draw object. Hold mouse button down and drag diagonally to opposite corner. When you release mouse button, object appears.

Use ▭ (rectangle tool) to draw figure at upper left.

Use ╲ (line tool) to draw first diagonal line at left in figure.

Use ◯ (oval tool) to draw third figure at left.

Use ↘ (arrow tool) to draw fourth figure at left.

> *Tip*
> *If you don't like the object you draw, tap* DELETE *to delete it. Then draw it again.*

4 ***Draw objects shown at right side of figure:***

Use same four tools, but this time hold SHIFT down as you drag pointer to draw each object. Keep holding SHIFT down until you release mouse button.

With line and arrow tools, SHIFT *forces line to be exactly horizontal, vertical, or diagonal. With other tools,* SHIFT *creates equal-sided object.*

5 ***Save changed Drawing file:***

On **File** menu, choose **Save**.

Select objects

Many commands act only upon selected objects. You can select one object or several objects at once.

1 **Select single objects on slide:**

Click pointer inside circle.

Click pointer inside square.

> *Handles show selected object.*

2 **Use selection marquee to select several objects:**

In slide area, position pointer between rectangle and square.

Press and drag diagonally so "marquee" (dashed outline) is like figure.

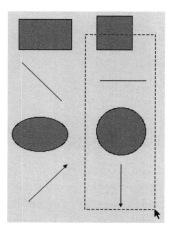

Release mouse button.

> *Only objects completely inside selection marquee are selected.*

By the way
Selection handles on shapes other than rectangles appear on an invisible bounding rectangle.

3 **Add objects to selection:**

Hold down SHIFT as you click rectangle and square.

4 **Remove object from selection:**

Hold down SHIFT as you click circle.

5 **Delete selected objects:**

On **Edit** menu, choose **Clear** (or tap DELETE).

6 **Undo change:**

On **Edit** menu, choose **Undo** (or tap ⌘ Z).

7 **Select all objects:**

On **Edit** menu, choose **Select All** (or tap ⌘ A).

8 **Deselect all selected objects:**

Click in slide area away from any object.

← *Complete previous activity before going on.*

Use line tools

In addition to the standard drawing tools, Microsoft PowerPoint provides special tools for more complex objects.

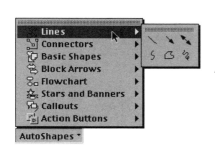

1 Add blank slide:

On **Insert** menu, choose **New Slide**. From **AutoLayout** icon list, choose layout named **Blank**. Click **OK**.

2 Display lines tools:

On drawing toolbar, display **AutoShapes** menu.

Highlight **Lines** on menu. Position pointer on hatched bar at top of submenu. Press and drag to "tear off" **Lines** palette.

3 Use scribble tool to draw curved lines:

On **Lines** palette, click 🖉 (scribble tool). Release mouse button.

Position pointer over drawing area. Press and drag to begin drawing object.

Pointer changes from crosshair to pencil shape.

Continue pressing and dragging to create object. Double-click mouse button to end drawing.

Object is selected. Same methods as before can be used to move, resize, reshape, or delete object.

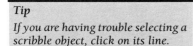

Tip
If you are having trouble selecting a scribble object, click on its line.

4 Use freeform tool to draw polygons:

On **Lines** palette, click ⬡ (freeform tool). Release mouse button.

Position pointer over clear part of slide area.

Click to establish starting point. Release mouse button.

Move pointer to new position and click to create first line.

Continue moving and clicking (not pressing!) to draw polygon.

Click starting point to close polygon or double-click to end.

Object is selected. Same methods as before can be used to move, resize, reshape, or delete object.

Tip
You can double-click to end the polygon at any point.

5 Combine methods in one object:

You can combine methods to create more complex objects. Move pointer and click to draw straight lines; drag to draw curves.

On **Lines** palette, click ⬡ (freeform tool). Release mouse button.

Freeform tool can create curved lines like scribble tool.

Try drawing ice cream cone in figure.

6 Close Lines palette:

Click ▣ (close box) in title bar of **Lines** palette.

7 Save file with new slide.

Use Basic Shapes tools

PowerPoint has two dozen drawing tools that automatically create complex, useful objects for your slides.

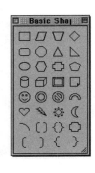

1 **Add new blank slide:**

On **Insert** menu, choose **New Slide**.

In **AutoLayout** window, choose **Blank**. Click **OK**.

2 **Display Basic Shapes palette:**

On drawing toolbar, display **AutoShapes** menu, choose **Basic Shapes**, and carefully drag hatched bar at top of submenu to tear off palette.

You can press and drag title bar to move palette where you want in window.

3 **Use Basic Shapes drawing tools:**

Click tool that looks like first object in figure below. Release mouse button.

Draw object on slide same way you drew rectangle on page 67.

Use tools on **Basic Shapes** palette to draw other objects in figure.

4 **Add new blank slide as in step 1.**

5 **Draw large cube:**

On **Basic Shapes** palette, click ▱ (cube tool). Release mouse button.

Position pointer over slide area. Press and drag diagonally, this time making cube larger. Release mouse button.

Notice adjustment handle just left of cube. Drag handle down to see effect.

6 **Close Basic Shapes palette:**

Click ▣ (close box) in title bar of **Basic Shapes** palette.

7 **Save file with two new slides.**

Duplicate objects

*Frequently you want multiple copies of the same object on a
slide. You can copy and paste or duplicate objects.*

1 *Create new blank slide:*

On **Insert** menu, choose **New Slide**. Double-click blank layout.

2 *Copy and paste object:*

Use 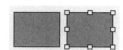 (rectangle tool) to draw small rectangle on left side of slide.

Make sure object is selected.

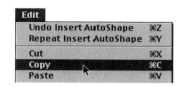

On **Edit** menu, choose **Copy** (or click 📋 in standard toolbar).

On **Edit** menu, choose **Paste** (or click 📋 in standard toolbar).

Copy appears slightly below and to right of original.

Move copy to right and line up with original.

On **Edit** menu, choose **Paste** again.

Another copy appears in same place as first copy originally appeared.

3 *Select and delete both copies.*

Original rectangle should remain on slide.

4 *Duplicate object:*

Select rectangle.

On **Edit** menu, choose **Duplicate**.

So far, effect is same as copying and pasting.

Move copy to right and line up with original.

On **Edit** menu, choose **Duplicate**.

*This duplicate is pasted in relation to second as you positioned second in
relation to original. Both object and its location are duplicated.*

On **Edit** menu, choose **Duplicate**.

*This duplicate is pasted in relation to third as third was pasted in relation
to second.*

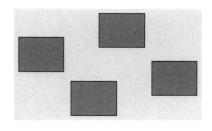

5 *Move rectangles:*

Move rectangles so they resemble figure to left.

6 *Save new file on floppy disk:*

On **File** menu, choose **Save**.

Save file with name **Objects**.

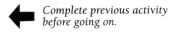
Attach text to objects

Frequently when you create an object, you put a label on it. In Microsoft PowerPoint, it's easy to attach the text to the object.

1 *Attach label to first rectangle:*

Select left rectangle.

> *White selection handles indicate object is selected.*

Type your first name.

Tap (ENTER) on numeric keypad (on right of keyboard) to end.

> *Name appears in middle of object. Thick, striped border appears.*

Move rectangle on slide.

> *Text moves with object. It is attached.*

Return rectangle to original location.

2 *Format attached text:*

With rectangle selected, click **B** (bold tool) on formatting toolbar.

On font size menu on formatting toolbar, choose **36**.

> *When whole object is selected, formatting applies to all attached text.*

3 *Edit attached text:*

Double-click your name in rectangle.

> *Text is highlighted.*

Type **1** and tap (ENTER) on numeric keypad (on far right of keyboard).

> *Entered text replaces highlighted text.*

4 *Add attached text to second rectangle:*

Select rectangle to right and type **2**.

Format same as text in first rectangle—bold, 36 point.

5 *Add attached text to third and fourth rectangles:*

Follow steps above to create following figure:

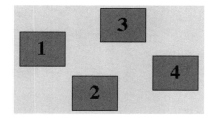

6 *Save changed Objects file.*

Complete previous activity before going on.

Change object fill

New PowerPoint objects are normally filled with a solid green.
You can modify the fill attribute in several ways.

1 **Change object fill (method 1):**

Select rectangle 1.

On drawing toolbar, click or press arrow at right side of 🎨 ▾ (fill color tool).

> *Colors directly under Automatic are from standard color scheme. To add colors to pop-up menu, you would choose* More Fill Colors.

On pop-up menu, choose **No Fill**.

> *Fill color is removed. Object is transparent.*

On drawing toolbar, click or press arrow at right side of 🎨 ▾. On pop-up menu, choose **Automatic**.

> *Standard (solid green) fill is added to object.*

2 **Change object fill (method 2):**

Make sure rectangle 1 is still selected.

On **Format** menu, choose **Colors and Lines**.

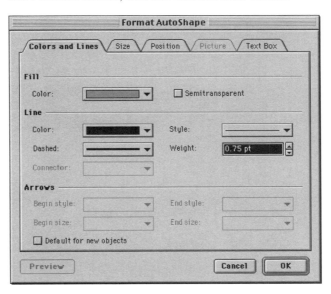

In **Fill** area, view **Color** pop-up menu.

> *Same items appear, but now you see more colors below standard eight.*

Choose red color.

Click **OK**.

> *Rectangle 1 is filled with solid red.*

3 **Change fill color of rectangle 2 to blue:**

Use method 2 above, but choose blue color.

Tip
Double-clicking an object also brings the Format AutoShape dialog box into view.

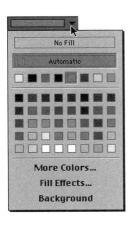

Tip
You can click the Preview button to see the effect without closing the dialog box. If you don't like the result, you can click Cancel. You may have to move the dialog box to see the result. Press and drag using the dialog box's title bar.

Change object fill   *continued*

4   **Change fill from solid to shaded:**

If necessary, select rectangle 2.

On drawing toolbar, click or press arrow at right side of 🖌 ▾.

On pop-up menu, choose **Fill Effects**.

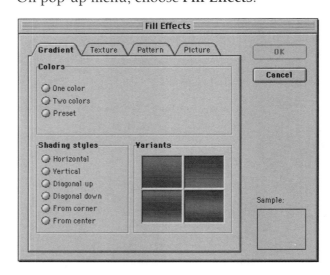

In **Colors** area, choose **One color**.

In **Shading styles** area, choose **From center**.

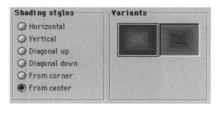

Click **OK** to see result.

5   **Add other fills:**

Select rectangle 3.

On drawing toolbar, click or press arrow at right side of 🖌 ▾.

On pop-up menu, choose **Fill Effects**.

Click **Pattern** tab to see patterned fills.

Choose one you like, then follow steps above to add patterned fill.

Select rectangle 4. Follow steps above to access fill effects.

Click **Texture** tab to see textured fills.

Choose one you like, then follow steps above to add textured fill.

6   **Save changed file.**

Complete previous activity before going on.

Change outline & shadow

In addition to modifying fills, you can change line colors, styles, and patterns; and you can add and adjust shadows.

Tip

If you remove both line and fill from an object, it can "disappear." If this happens, on the Edit *menu, choose* Select All *to see the selection handles of the missing object.*

By the way

You can also use the Colors and Lines *tab of the* Format AutoShapes *dialog box (see figure on page 77) to change outline properties. All the toolbar pop-up menus used here also appear on that tab.*

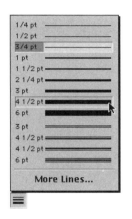

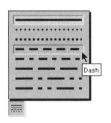

1 **Switch object outline off and back on:**

Select rectangle 1.

On drawing toolbar, click or press arrow at right side of 🖌▾ (line color tool).

On pop-up menu, choose **No Line**.

Outline is removed from object.

Click right side of 🖌▾ again. Choose **Automatic**.

Standard (black) outline is added to object.

2 **Change line width of rectangle 3:**

Select rectangle 3.

On drawing toolbar, click or press ≣ (line style tool).

On pop-up menu, choose solid line labeled **4 1/2 pt**.

Outline border of rectangle 3 displays wider border. (It's not as wide as on pop-up menu because you're seeing slide at reduced view scale.)

3 **Change line style of rectangle 4:**

Select rectangle 4. Use above steps to change outline to solid 6-point line.

On drawing toolbar, click or press ▦ (dash style tool).

On pop-up menu, choose fourth format (see figure).

Outline is thick and dashed.

Change outline & shadow *continued*

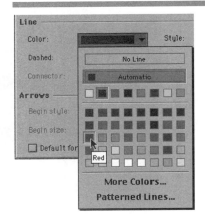

4 *Change line color:*

Make sure rectangle 4 is still selected.

On **Format** menu, choose **Colors and Lines**.

In **Line** area, show **Color** pop-up menu and choose red color.

Click **OK**.

5 *Add shadow to object:*

Select rectangle 1.

On drawing toolbar, click or press ▣ (shadow tool).

On pop-up menu, choose ▣ (shadow style 6 tool).

Click outside rectangle to see shadow.

6 *Change shadow color:*

Select rectangle 1 again.

On drawing toolbar, view shadow menu again and choose **Shadow Settings**.

> *Settings palette appears:*

On palette, click or press right side of ▣▾ (shadow color tool).

> *Color pop-up menu appears:*

Choose black color (either one will work).

7 *Increase shadow offset:*

On **Shadow Settings** palette, use ▣▣▣▣ (nudge buttons) to increase or decrease offset of shadow in direction of arrow.

Click ▣ to close **Shadow Settings** palette.

Deselect rectangle 1 to see result.

8 *Save changed file.*

Complete previous activity before going on.

Align objects

Microsoft PowerPoint allows you to line objects up with one another on their top, bottom, middle, left, center, or right edges.

1 Select all rectangles.

You must select objects you wish to line up.

2 Align objects by bottom edges:

On drawing toolbar, view **Draw** menu. Choose **Align or Distribute**, and carefully drag submenu off as palette.

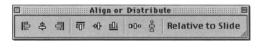

Click ▣ (align bottom tool).

All rectangles are now lined up with bottom edge of rectangle 2.

> **By the way**
>
> *In this example, all objects are the same size, so results are the same whether you align on tops, bottoms, or middles.*

"Bottommost" object defines location of alignment.

3 Undo alignment change:

On **Edit** menu, choose **Undo Align Object**.

4 Align objects by top edges:

On **Align or Distribute** palette, click ▣ (align top tool).

All rectangles are now lined up with top edge of rectangle 3. "Topmost" object defines location of alignment.

> **Tip**
>
> *To control where objects line up, move one object to the desired location; then select all and use the Align command.*

5 Undo alignment:

On **Edit** menu, choose **Undo Align Object**.

6 Align objects by left edges:

On **Align or Distribute** palette, click ▣ (align left tool).

All rectangles are now lined up with left edge of rectangle 1. "Leftmost" object defines location of alignment.

Undo alignment.

7 Align objects by right edges:

On **Align or Distribute** palette, click ▣ (align right tool).

All rectangles are now lined up with right edge of rectangle 4. "Rightmost" object defines location of alignment.

8 Undo alignment. Close Align or Distribute palette.

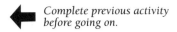
Change stacking order

Each new object is on a layer in front of the rest of the objects, but you can change the order of the layers.

1 **Add blank slide:**

On **Insert** menu, choose **New Slide**. Choose layout named **Blank**. Click **OK**.

2 **Create objects in order shown in figure below:**

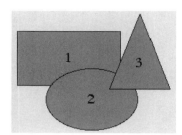

> *By the way*
> Create objects in the order in which they are numbered. If you want to add numbers, see steps on page 76.

It is not necessary to add numbers to figures.

Note stacking order.

Each new object is on layer in front of other object(s).

3 **Tear off Order palette and move triangle behind oval:**

Select triangle if it does not already have handles.

On drawing toolbar, view **Draw** menu. Choose **Order**, and carefully drag submenu off as palette.

On **Order** palette, click 🔲 (send backward tool).

> *Layer with triangle is now behind oval but still in front of rectangle.*

> *By the way*
> You can also use the commands from the pop-up menu without floating the Order palette.

4 **Move oval layer behind all other objects:**

Select oval. On **Order** palette, click 🔲 (send to back tool).

> *Layer with oval is now behind others.*

5 **Move oval layer in front of all other objects:**

On **Order** palette, click 🔲 (bring to front tool).

> *Layer with oval is now in front.*

6 **Move rectangle one layer forward:**

Select rectangle. On **Order** palette, click 🔲 (bring forward tool).

> *Layer with rectangle is now in front of triangle but behind oval.*

7 **Use any commands to return layers to original order.**

8 **Close Order palette. Save and close file.**

9 **Quit Microsoft PowerPoint.**

Create presentation

Now you will create a slide presentation using PowerPoint. You will begin with a new file.

1 **Start Microsoft PowerPoint as on page 64.**

2 **Create new blank presentation:**

In **Create a new presentation using** area, choose **Blank presentation**. Click **OK**.

3 **Choose layout of first slide:**

Selected layout is Title Slide. This is usually best for first slide.

Selected layout ——— 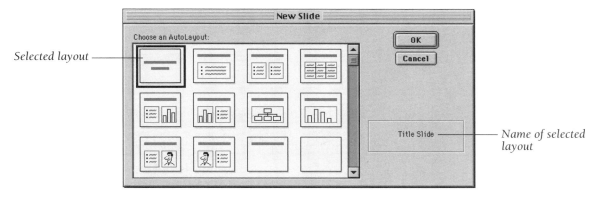 ——— Name of selected layout

Click any AutoLayout icon to see its name at lower right of dialog box.

Use vertical scroll bar to see all 24 ready-made layouts.

Scroll back to top and click icon for **Title Slide** layout. Click **OK**.

4 **View Microsoft PowerPoint document window:**

Slide you're creating ——— 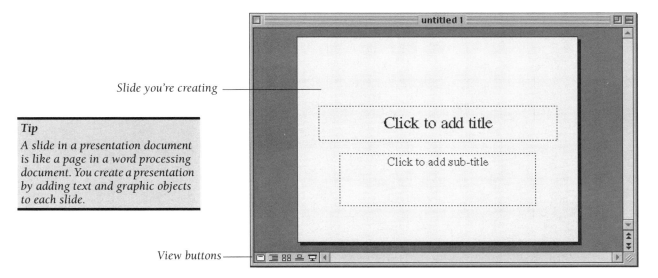 ——— View buttons

Tip
A slide in a presentation document is like a page in a word processing document. You create a presentation by adding text and graphic objects to each slide.

5 **Set up toolbars:**

Use **Toolbars** submenu on **View** menu, if necessary, to show standard, formatting, and drawing toolbars.

Close **Common Tasks** palette, if present.

Create presentation   *continued*

By the way
Many of the tools on the standard and formatting toolbars are identical with those on the same toolbars in Microsoft Word and Microsoft Excel.

6 **Explore tools on standard and formatting toolbars:**

Move pointer to each tool icon. Read name below pointer.

Standard toolbar contains tools for working with presentations. Formatting toolbar contains tools for formatting text.

7 **Look at view buttons (at bottom left of window).**

Highlighted button is for slide view, which is current view. View buttons allow you to see same presentation document in many different ways.

8 **Note number of current slide and name of current presentation design in status bar.**

Presentation document can have many slides. Label at left shows which slide you are viewing and working on. Label at right shows name of design.

9 **Note boxes on slide 1.**

Boxes on slide 1 are text boxes. Labels in boxes are placeholders for text you will enter next.

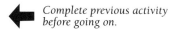

Complete previous activity before going on.

Add text to slide

AutoLayout slides come with placeholders for text and other objects. The next step now is to replace the placeholders.

1 *Replace title placeholder:*

Click I-beam pointer anywhere inside top placeholder box on slide.

> *Text goes away and blinking insertion point appears in box.*

Type **Petal Pushers Flower Shop**.

Click white background area away from any text.

> *You have replaced title placeholder with your own text.*

2 *Replace subtitle placeholder:*

Click I-beam pointer anywhere inside bottom placeholder box.

> *Text goes away and insertion point appears.*

Type **Local, National, and International Flower and Plant Deliveries**.

> *Note that text "wraps" (moves to next line) within margins set by box.*

By the way
You can also tap RETURN *to force line breaks where you want them.*

3 *See results:*

Click white background area away from text.

> *Finished slide appears with no dotted placeholder boundaries. Once placeholders are gone, slide is just like one you could have created from blank layout by drawing text boxes (using text box tool* 🖾 *on drawing toolbar).*

> Petal Pushers Flower Shop
>
> Local, National, and International
> Flower and Plant Deliveries

4 *Correct any mistakes:*

If you made any typing error, move pointer over it on slide.

> *Pointer shape changes to I-beam when over text.*

Click just right of error and make necessary corrections.

> *Tap* DELETE *to erase; type characters to add.*

Click white background area outside placeholders when finished.

By the way
Microsoft Office applications display a zig zag red line under any word they consider misspelled.

Save file & insert new slide

After creating a new presentation document, you should save it permanently on disk. Adding new slides is easy!

1 **Save new file with name Slides on floppy disk:**

Follow steps on page 66, but type **Slides** as file name.

2 **Add second slide to presentation:**

On **Insert** menu, choose **New Slide**.

> *New Slide dialog box appears, this time with Bulleted List layout selected as type for slide 2. That's usually a good choice.*

Click **OK**.

> *Slide 2 is added and appears with two text placeholders.*

3 **Enter text for slide 2:**

Click title placeholder and type **Welcome**.

Click text placeholder and type **What Can Petal Pushers Do for You?**

Tap (RETURN) now to begin new paragraph.

Type your name, comma, space, and **President**.

> *Each line has bullet mark to left.*

By the way
Microsoft PowerPoint normally puts a wavy red line under any word it considers misspelled.

4 **View slide 2:**

Click in white area outside placeholders.

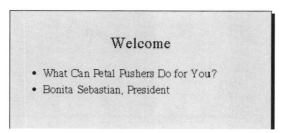

Welcome

- What Can Petal Pushers Do for You?
- Bonita Sebastian, President

5 **Correct any errors.**

6 **Save file with new slide:**

On **File** menu, choose **Save** (or click on standard toolbar).

Complete previous activity before going on.

Add slides in outline view

If many of your slides will be bulleted or numbered lists, you can add and edit them most easily in "outline" view.

1 *Change to outline view:*

Click ≡ (outline view button) at lower left of window.

Note how two slides appear in outline view:

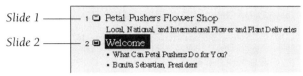

Slide 1 — 1 ▭ Petal Pushers Flower Shop
        Local, National, and International Flower and Plant Deliveries
Slide 2 — 2 ▣ Welcome
      • What Can Petal Pushers Do for You?
      • Bonita Sebastian, President

Move pointer to outline toolbar (normally at left edge of screen). For each tool, read name below pointer.

← — *Promote*
→ — *Demote*
↑ — *Move Up*
↓ — *Move Down*
− — *Collapse*
+ — *Expand*
≡ — *Collapse All*
≡ — *Expand All*
ᴬ◿ — *Show/Hide Formatting*

2 *Create new slide:*

Click to right of last line of text.

Tap [RETURN] to begin new paragraph.

> *Oops! You don't want new bulleted item. You want new slide.*

On outline toolbar, click ← (promote tool).

> *Slide 3 is added. Layout is automatically same as previous slide.*

3 *Enter title on slide 3 in outline view:*

Type **Topics** and tap [RETURN].

> *Oops! New slide 4 is automatically added. But you haven't added bulleted list for slide 3 yet!*

4 *Add bulleted list for slide 3:*

Click → (demote tool) on outline toolbar (or tap [TAB]).

> *Slide 4 is gone. Bullet appears, and insertion point moves to right.*

Type **Services** and tap [RETURN].

> *Insertion point moves down to next line at same indent level. Outlines work same way in PowerPoint and Word.*

Type **Delivery Options** and tap [RETURN].

Type **Geographical Coverage**. Do *not* tap [RETURN] now.

> *Line is last of bulleted list on slide 3.*

1 ▭ Petal Pushers Flower Shop
    Local, National, and International Flower and Plant Deliveries
2 ▭ Welcome
    • What Can Petal Pushers Do for You?
    • Bonita Sebastian, President
3 ▭ Topics
    • Services
    • Delivery Options
    • Geographical Coverage

By the way

In outline view, a miniature of the current slide normally appears on a palette. This allows you to see how the text will look and to make changes, such as shortening lines for better fit.

5 *Create slide 4:*

Tap (RETURN).

> *Oops again! New bulleted item appears. You wanted new slide.*

Click ◆ (promote tool) on outline toolbar or tap (SHIFT)(TAB).

> *Slide 4 appears. Bullet is gone, and insertion point moves to left.*

Type **Services** as title.

Tap (RETURN), then click ➡ (demote tool) or tap (TAB).

Using methods above, add bulleted list shown below.

Tip

Text can also be entered in slide view. Entering text in outline view is sometimes easier because you can see all the slides at once.

4 ▢ Services
  • Flowers
  • Plants
  • Arrangements of All Types
  • Subscription Services
  • Customized Options of All Kinds

6 *Create slides 5 and 6:*

Using methods above, create slides 5 and 6 in outline view.

> *Finished slides 5 and 6 should look like this:*

5 ▢ Delivery Options
  • One-Time
  • Subscription
6 ▢ Geographical Coverage
  • Local
  • National
  • International

7 *Return to slide view and see results:*

Click ▢ (slide view button) at lower left of window.

Notice previous slide and next slide buttons below vertical scroll bar.

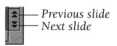 — *Previous slide*
— *Next slide*

Click buttons to see all slides in presentation.

8 *Save Slides presentation file:*

Use previous slide button to return to slide 1.

On **File** menu, choose **Save**.

> *You'll be using file you created many times in future activities.*

If you're not going on right now, choose **Quit** on **File** menu.

View & modify slide show

You can add effects to a presentation that you display on your computer monitor or through a projection device.

1 *View slide show presentation:*

If necessary, open presentation file **Slides** from your floppy disk.

Click ⊑ (slide show button) at bottom of window.

Presentation begins, with slide 1 filling screen.

Tap (SPACEBAR) or mouse button to move to next slide. Repeat until you've seen whole presentation and **PowerPoint** window returns.

2 *Switch to slide sorter view:*

Click ⊞ (slide sorter view button) to switch to new view of presentation.

You see all slides as if on light table. New toolbar appears at top.

Put pointer on each item in slide sorter toolbar to see its name.

3 *Add transition effect to slide 1:*

If necessary, click slide 1 to select it.

At left of new toolbar, click ⊡ (slide transition tool) to see dialog box.

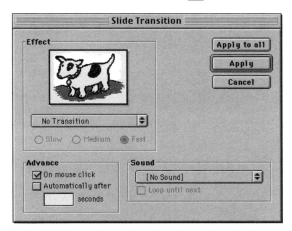

Watch sample. On **Effect** pop-up list, choose **Split Vertical Out**.

From the three speed options, choose **Slow**.

Click **Apply**. Don't click **Apply to All**!

4 *Add different transition and sound to slide 2:*

Click slide 2 image.

Click ⊡ to display **Slide Transition** dialog box again.

On **Effect** list, choose **Fade Through Black**. Choose **Slow**.

On **Sound** list, choose **Clapping**.

Click **Apply**.

5 *Add transitions to many slides at once:*

Still in slide sorter view, click slide 3 image.

With (SHIFT) held down, click slides 4, 5, and 6.

Click 🖻 to display **Slide Transition** dialog box.

On **Effect** list, choose **Wipe Left**.

Choose **Medium** from the three speed options.

Click **Apply**.

6 *Add animation to slides:*

Slides 3, 4, 5, and 6 should still be selected. If not, select them.

Click or press ▾ to see **Text Body Animation** list.

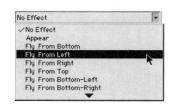

Choose **Fly from Left**.

7 *View slide show with effects:*

Click to select slide 1 so slide show will begin there.

Click 🖵 (slide show button) at bottom of window.

> *Screen opens black, then splits vertically to reveal slide 1.*

Move mouse.

Click ✍ △ icon at lower left of screen.

On pop-up menu, choose **Pen**.

> *(Choose* Pointer Options, Pen Color *on same menu to change pen color.)*

Draw line under title.

Tap (SPACEBAR), (↓), or (PAGE DOWN) to move to next slide.

> *Screen fades to black, then slide 2 appears.*

Tap (↑), or (PAGE UP) to move to previous slide.

Go forward through whole slide show.

> *Notice slides 3, 4, 5, and 6 grow by animated bullet by bullet on screen.*

8 *Close presentation file without saving changes:*

On **File** menu, choose **Close**.

Click **Don't Save** when asked whether to save changes.

By the way

Text body animation, sometimes called a build, is usually used on a slide with multiple bullets. Items appear one at a time as if they were on individual slides.

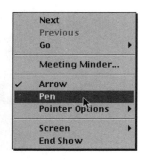

Tip

You can go to directly to any slide by typing the slide number and tapping (RETURN). *You can end a slide show any time by tapping* (ESC).

STOP *Slides file as completed on page 88 must be on floppy disk.*

Check spelling

Microsoft PowerPoint can check the spelling in a presentation and add new words to your custom dictionary.

By the way

If no words are misspelled, the Spelling dialog box does not open at all. Only the message box in step 5 appears.

1 *Open presentation file Slides from your floppy disk:*

With disk in drive, choose **Slides** on **File** menu.

2 *Begin spelling check:*

On **Tools** menu, choose **Spelling**.

> *If Microsoft PowerPoint detects errors,* Spelling *dialog box appears:*

3 *Change any misspelled words:*

In **Suggestions** list, click to highlight desired replacement word.

Click **Change**.

> *You can click* Change All *to replace all occurrences of misspelled word in entire presentation.*

4 *Work with flagged proper names:*

If your name is flagged by spelling checker, click **Ignore**.

> *You can click* Ignore All *to skip other occurrences of flagged word in entire presentation.*

OR

Click **Add** to include name in custom dictionary so it will never be flagged again.

5 *End spelling check:*

> *When spelling check is finished, message box appears:*

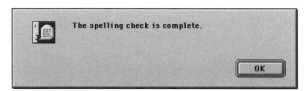

Click **OK**.

6 *Save presentation file with changes:*

On **File** menu, choose **Save**.

View slides in slide view

When working on a presentation in slide view, you need to be able to move from slide to slide and make changes.

1 **View presentation in slide view:**

If necessary, click [] (slide view button) to left of horizontal scroll bar.

When in slide view, button appears depressed and is darker than others.

Tip
Pay close attention to the view buttons. The button for the view you're using looks pushed in and is darker than the rest.

2 **Move to last slide in presentation:**

Tap [⌘] [END].

3 **Move directly to slide 1.**

Tap [⌘] [HOME].

4 **View slides one at a time (method 1):**

Tap [PAGE DOWN] to go to next slide.

Continue to tap [PAGE DOWN], reviewing each slide until you reach last slide.

Tap [PAGE UP] until you reach slide 1.

All above keyboard commands also work in slide show view.

5 **View slides one at a time (method 2):**

Click next slide button (below vertical scroll bar).

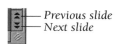
— Previous slide
— Next slide

Continue to click next slide button, until you reach last slide.

Click previous slide button on vertical scroll bar.

Next to last slide appears.

6 **Move to slide 1:**

Press and drag scroll box to top of vertical scroll bar.

Notice slide indicator near arrow as you drag.

Slide: 1 of 6
Petal Pushers Flower Shop

Edit & rearrange text

Text can be edited in slide view or outline view. You can also easily rearrange the order of bullets on a slide in either view.

1   **If necessary, open Slides file from your floppy disk.**

2   **Edit text on slide 1 in slide view:**

If necessary, click ▣ (slide view button) at lower left of window.

If necessary, tap ⌘ HOME to move to slide 1.

Click to put insertion point after **s** in **deliveries**. Tap DELETE three times to delete last three characters. Type **y Services**.

Text of slide 1 should now look like this:

> ### Petal Pushers Flower Shop
>
> Local, National, and International
> Flower and Plant Delivery Services

3   **Change to outline view:**

Click ▤ (outline view button).

Change you made appears in every view.

4   **Rearrange bulleted lines on slide 2 in outline view:**

Click in bulleted line containing your name.

Position pointer over bullet mark at left side of text.

Watch for pointer to change shape: ⊹

Press and drag up to move text under title of slide:

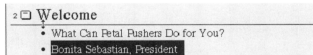

Note horizontal line across page marking new location.

When line is at correct location, release mouse button.

Bulleted line moves to new location.

5   **Add bulleted line to slide 2 in outline view:**

Click to right of **You?** in second bulleted line.

Tap RETURN.

New bulleted line is created.

Type **What Can You Do for Petal Pushers?**

By the way
You can also move lines up or down with the move-up and move-down tools on the outline toolbar. See figure in margin on page 87.

6 *Add new level of bullets to slide 5:*

In outline view, locate slide 5.

Click to put insertion point just right of **Subscription**.

Tap RETURN .

> *New bulleted line at same level is created.*

On outline toolbar, click ➡ (demote tool) or tap TAB .

> *New line is indented one more level. Note different bullet mark.*

Type **Daily** and tap RETURN .

> *Another bulleted line at new level is created.* RETURN *always creates new line at same level as line above.*

Enter remaining lines as shown in figure.

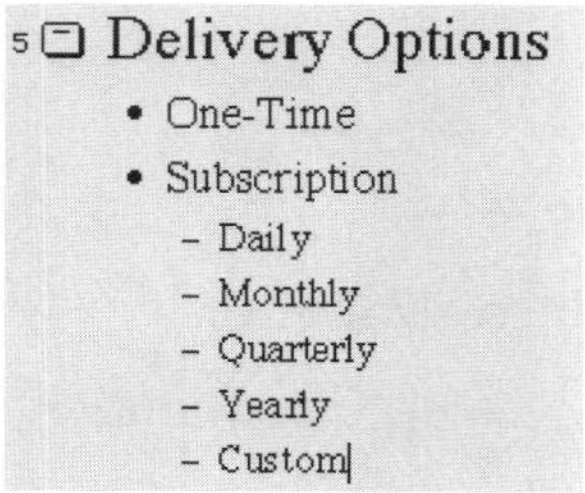

> 5 ☐ Delivery Options
> - One-Time
> - Subscription
>   - Daily
>   - Monthly
>   - Quarterly
>   - Yearly
>   - Custom|

7 *Review edited presentation in slide view:*

Click ☐ to change to slide view.

> *Current slide appears in slide view.*

> **Delivery Options**
> - One-Time
> - Subscription
>   - Daily
>   - Monthly
>   - Quarterly
>   - Yearly
>   - Custom

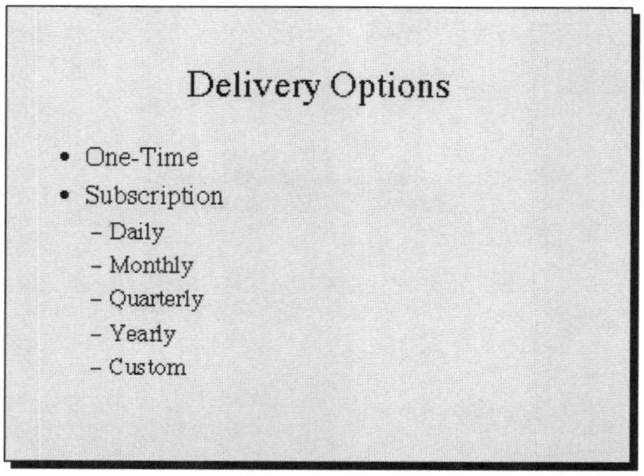

Tap ⌘ HOME to move to slide 1.

Tap PAGE DOWN to browse though slides one at a time.

Make any desired or necessary changes.

Tap ⌘ HOME to move back to slide 1 again.

8 *Close presentation file without saving changes.*

Slides file as completed on page 88 must be on floppy disk.

STOP

Rearrange slides

After reviewing slides you may wish to rearrange the order in which information is presented.

1 **Open Slides file from your floppy disk.**

2 **Switch to slide sorter view:**

Click ⊞ (slide sorter view button) at bottom left of window.

Slides appear in miniature, as if on light table.

By the way
Your screen may not look exactly like this one. The display will depend on the type of monitor and the current view percentage.

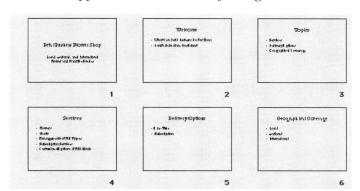

3 *Change order of slides (method 1, slide view):*

Put pointer on slide 6 and drag to left of slide 4.

Note pointer shape and dotted-line position marker.

When position marker is to left of slide 4, release mouse button.

Slide 6 becomes slide 4. Slides 4 and 5 become slides 5 and 6.

4 *Change order of slides (method 2, outline view):*

Click ▤ (outline view button) at bottom left of window.

Outline shows new order. Order of slides is same in all views.

Put pointer at small slide icon to left of slide 3 title.

Press mouse button and drag up until long horizontal line is just above slide 2 title.

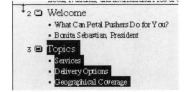

Release mouse button.

Slides 2 and 3 swap places.

5 **If you're not continuing, close presentation file without saving changes.**

STOP *Slides file as completed on page 88 must be on floppy disk.*

Delete slide

Sometimes you simply want to get rid of a slide in your presentation. That's easy to do (and undo).

1 **Delete slide (method 1, outline view):**

If necessary, open **Slides** from your floppy disk and click 🔳 to switch to outline view.

Position pointer over tiny slide icon for slide 1.

Pointer changes shape: .

Tap mouse button.

Entire slide is selected.

Tap DELETE .

Slide is deleted from presentation file.

By the way
You can also use the Cut or Clear commands on the Edit menu to delete a slide.

---

2 **Undo action (method 1):**

On **Edit** menu, choose **Undo Clear**.

Slide is "undeleted." Most PowerPoint actions can be undone.

3 **Delete slide (method 2, slide sorter view):**

Click 🔳 (slide sorter view button) at bottom left of window.

Click to select slide 3.

Tap DELETE .

Slide 3 is deleted.

By the way
You can click the arrow on the side of the undo tool to display a list of multiple actions you can undo.

---

4 **Undo action (method 2):**

Click 🔙 (undo tool) on standard toolbar.

Slide 3 reappears.

5 **Delete slide (method 3, slide view):**

Click 🔲 (slide view button) at bottom left of window.

Tap PAGE UP to see slide 2.

On **Edit** menu, choose **Delete Slide**.

In slide view, this is only way to delete slides.

6 **Undo action (method 3):**

Tap ⌘ Z .

Slide 2 reappears.

7 **Close presentation file without saving changes.**

Change fonts, sizes & styles

Using familiar tools, you can easily change the appearance of any text you select on a slide.

1 Open Slides file from your floppy disk.

2 View slide 1 in slide view:

If necessary, click ⬚ to switch to slide view. Tap (⌘)(HOME) to see slide 1.

3 Check current font, size, and style of title:

Highlight any text in title.

On formatting toolbar, view current font (**Times**), size (**44** point), and style (none—no bold, italic, underline, or shadow).

4 Change font, size, and style of title:

Click border of title text box to select whole box as graphic object.

On **Format** menu, choose **Font**. Again notice current formats.

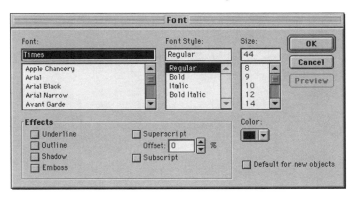

On **Font** list, choose **Helvetica**.

On **Font Style** list, choose **Bold**.

On **Size** list, choose **60**.

In **Effects** area, click **Shadow** to put mark in check box.

Click **OK**.

Changes affect all text in box. Title now wraps to second line.

On formatting toolbar, select **44** on font size list.

Title no longer wraps.

5 Change selected text in title:

Highlight **Petal Pushers** in title box.

On formatting toolbar, click *I* (italic tool).

Only highlighted text is changed.

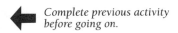
Use slide master

Every presentation has a "slide master." Format changes you make here affect all slides you haven't already formatted.

1 Switch to view of slide master:

On **View** menu, choose **Master**. On submenu, choose **Slide Master**.

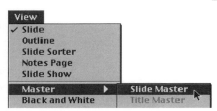

Slide master and Master palette appear. You see placeholders for formatting text on all slides.

2 Format title on slide master to change format on all slides:

Tap TAB to select first text block (title of slide).

> **Tip**
> *The patterned border you now see means the whole text block is selected.*

On **Format** menu, choose **Font**.

Change font to **Helvetica** and add **Bold** style.

In **Effects** area, click **Shadow**. Click **OK**.

3 Format body text on slide master:

Tap TAB to select next text block (object area).

> **Tip**
> *You can also use tools on the formatting toolbar to apply these formats.*

Use formatting toolbar to change font to **Helvetica** and add **Bold** style.

4 Change size of text within body:

Click anywhere in first bulleted line.

On formatting toolbar, select **24** on font size list.

> *Text size is changed for first-level items only.*

5 See results:

Click **Close** on **Master** palette.

View slide show. Use PAGE DOWN to see each slide.

> *All slides now have formats you gave to slide master.*

6 Close presentation file without saving changes.

STOP *Slides file as completed on page 88 must be on floppy disk.*

Create slide with graph

You can add a graph to a slide. Creating a graph in Microsoft PowerPoint is similar to creating it in Microsoft Excel.

1 **Open Slides presentation.**

2 **Add new slide with graph layout:**

If necessary, click ☐ to go to slide view.

Tap ⌘ END to go to last slide.

On **Insert** menu, choose **New Slide**. In **AutoLayout** list, click **Chart** icon (second row, fourth column).

> **Tip**
>
> *You can also create a graph on any slide by using the* Insert Chart *tool on the standard toolbar or the* Insert Chart *menu command.*

Click **OK**.

3 **Add title:**

Click title placeholder and type **Flower Sales**.

4 **Open Microsoft Graph:**

Double-click graph placeholder.

> *In time, two new windows appear. Windows belong to Microsoft Graph.*

Look at names in menu bar near top of screen. Look at toolbar.

> *Data and* Chart *menus are new.* Slide Show *menu is gone. Items on menus are also changed. Menu bar and toolbar now belong to Microsoft Graph.*

Click **Datasheet** window to activate it.

> *Datasheet holds data for graph. You'll replace default data with your data.*

Carefully resize window as in figure so you can see graph.

Double click to add chart

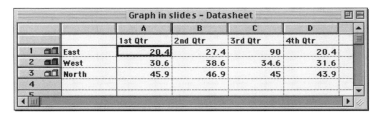

5 **Enter category labels:**

Click to select cell in row 1 containing word **East**.

Type **Rose** and tap RETURN.

> *Active cell is now* West.

Type **Pansy** and tap RETURN.

> *Active cell is now* North.

Type **Tulip** and tap RETURN. Notice changes in legend beside graph.

Create slide with graph *continued*

6 *Enter series labels:*

Click to select cell containing words **1st Qtr**.

Type **1995** and tap TAB.

> *Active cell is now* 2nd Qtr.

Type **1996** and tap TAB to move to next cell to right.

Type **1997** and tap RETURN to end text entry.

7 *Enter data:*

Watch columns on graph as you select cells and add data shown in figure.

		A	B	C	D	
		1995	1996	1997	4th Qtr	
1	Rose	123	234	345	20.4	
2	Pansy	147	258	369	31.6	
3	Tulip	159	269	248	43.9	
4						
5						

Graph in slides – Datasheet

8 *Remove column D data from graph:*

Double-click [D] (header of column D).

> *Data is dimmed in window and disappears from graph.*

9 *Move Datasheet window to back and see whole slide:*

On **View** menu, choose **Datasheet**.

> *Selecting* Datasheet *again (or* 🔲 *on graph toolbar) brings window back.*

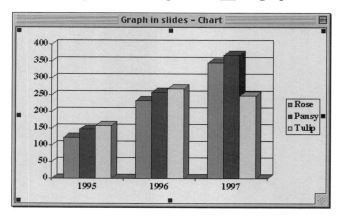

10 *Close Microsoft Graph:*

On **File** menu, choose **Quit and Return to Slides**.

> *PowerPoint menus and toolbars reappear. Graph remains on slide.*

11 *Save presentation file.*

← *Complete previous activity before going on.*

Format graph

Graphs in Microsoft PowerPoint can be formatted using methods similar to those used in Microsoft Excel.

1 **Open Microsoft Graph:**

Double-click anywhere inside graph area.

> *Datasheet, graph toolbar, and menus appear.*

2 **Add label to value axis:**

On **Chart** menu, choose **Chart Options**.

Tip

This dialog box allows you to put a title on the graph. However, it is best to put the title on the slide (as you did earlier). There's more space, and the title will not change size with the graph.

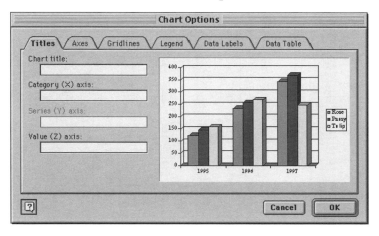

Click text box for **Value (Z) axis**.

Type **Dozen**. Click **OK**.

Tip

Do not click outside graph area on slide. If you do, you will return to Microsoft PowerPoint application. If this happens, double-click graph to return to Microsoft Graph application.

3 **Format axis title:**

Double-click new **Dozen** label.

In **Format Axis Title** dialog box, click **Alignment** tab.

In **Orientation** area, drag red diamond to top (see figure).

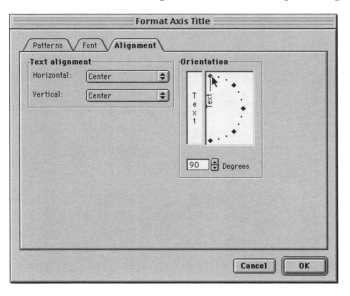

Click **OK**.

4 *Remove border from legend and put legend at bottom:*

Double-click legend (at right of graph).

Click **Patterns** tab. In **Border** area, click **None**.

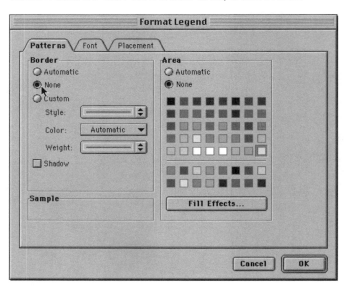

Click **Placement** tab. In **Type** area, click **Bottom**. Click **OK**.

5 *Change data being graphed:*

If necessary, click 🖩 (view datasheet tool) on graph toolbar.

Click cell C3 containing 1997 sales of tulips.

Type **348** and tap RETURN.

Click view datasheet tool again to move to back.

6 *View finished graph:*

On **File** menu, choose **Quit and Return to Slides**.

> *You exit Microsoft Graph application and return to Microsoft PowerPoint.*

Tip

The graph is now an object on the slide. It can be deleted, moved, or resized using the same techniques used with other objects. See page 68.

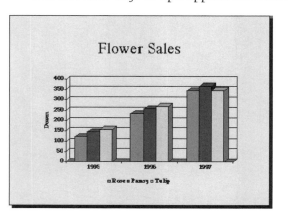

7 *Save presentation with new slide.*

A presentation file must be open in slide view.

Add clip art

You can add a ready-made graphic to a slide. Microsoft Office contains a gallery of clip art you can use.

1 **Create new slide:**

On **Insert** menu, choose **New Slide**.

From **AutoLayout** list, select **Text & Clip Art** (third row, first column).

Click **OK**.

Click title placeholder. Type **Flowers for Every Occasion**.

2 **Open and view Clip Gallery:**

Double-click clip art placeholder.

Tip

You can also add clip art to a slide using the Insert Clip Art *tool on the standard toolbar or the* Insert Clip Art *menu command. See next page.*

Double click to add clip art

By the way

The amount of clip art displayed in the gallery is determined by the installation. If you do not have the entire collection, substitute other images.

The first time the ClipArt Gallery is opened, a dialog box may appear asking whether to add new images. If this happens, you can say yes. Be aware, however, that the process takes time.

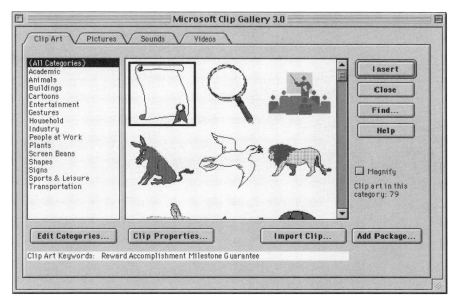

Click category name in list. Scroll through new images that appear.

Click **Find** button to open dialog box for locating clip art.

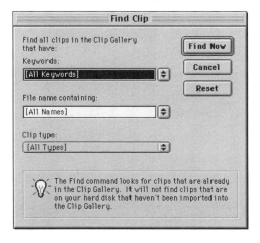

Add clip art *continued*

3 *Find picture of flower:*

If necessary, click text box for entering keyword.

Type **flower** and click **Find Now**.

Image with flower appears. (It may not be same as figure below.)

Click **Insert** to accept clip art and add it to slide.

Tip

The clip art is now an object on the slide. It can be deleted, moved, or resized using the same techniques used with other objects. See page 68.

4 *View picture toolbar:*

Put pointer on buttons and read descriptions.

Picture toolbar contains buttons for options to modify picture.

No picture toolbar?

If picture toolbar does not appear when graphic is selected, on View *menu, choose* Toolbars *and from submenu, choose* Picture.

5 *Add clip art to existing slide without placeholder:*

If you're using file **Slides**, use (PAGE UP) to go to slide 6. Otherwise go to any other slide in file, or add new blank slide.

On **Insert** menu, choose **Picture**, then **Clip Art**.

Use steps above to find and insert plane or ship.

Once image is on slide, adjust its size and move it to desired location.

Finished slide should look similar to this:

Tip

To exchange one clip art image for another, double-click the image to reopen the ClipArt Gallery.

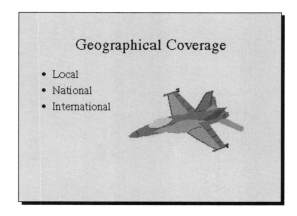

6 *Save presentation.*

Add footer & graphic to master

Frequently you want a label or graphic on all slides in a presentation. Just add the label or graphic to the slide master.

1 *Move to slide master view:*

On **View** menu, choose **Master**; on submenu, choose **Slide Master**.

2 *Enter text:*

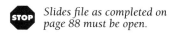

On master, click **Footer Area** text box.

Type **Petal Pushers Flower Shop**.

Click outside text box to end editing.

3 *Format text:*

Click to border of footer area text box.

On formatting toolbar, choose **Helvetica** from font list.

On formatting toolbar, choose **14** from font size list.

4 *View footer text on slides:*

Return to slide view.

Tap `PAGE UP` and `PAGE DOWN` keys to review slides. Note footer text.

5 *Switch back to slide master:*

With `SHIFT` held down, click ☐ (slide view button).

> *That's quick way to go to slide master view.*

6 *Add graphic object to slide master:*

On **Insert** menu, choose **Picture**, then **Clip Art**.

Use steps on page 103 to locate and insert appropriate graphic image.

7 *Resize and position object in upper right corner as in figure.*

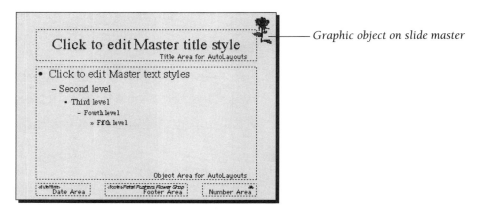

— *Graphic object on slide master*

8 *View text and graphic object on all slides:*

Click 🔲 (slide view button) to return to slide view.

Review slides using PAGE UP and PAGE DOWN.

9 *Suppress display of slide master objects on one slide:*

Move to slide 8.

On **Format** menu, choose **Background**.

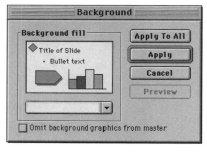

Click to place mark in **Omit background graphics from master**.

Click **Apply**.

10 *View presentation using slide show:*

On **Slide Show** menu, choose **View Show** (or go to slide 1 and click 🖥).

Click mouse button to advance from slide to slide.

11 *When show has ended, close presentation without saving changes.*

STOP *Slides file as completed on page 88 must be on floppy disk.*

Apply presentation design

Microsoft PowerPoint contains built-in color and black-and-white templates for slide shows, overheads, and slides.

1 **Open Slides file.**

2 **View available design templates:**

On **Format** menu, choose **Apply Design**.

In **Templates** list, choose **Presentation Designs**.

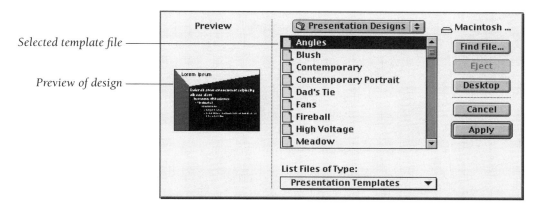

Selected template file

Preview of design

Click first design name. Use ⊽ and ⬆ to scroll through list of available designs and see previews at left.

3 **Apply design:**

Highlight name of design you want to use.

Click **Apply**.

By the way
Applying a design creates a new slide master with all the format details. Any previous slide master changes you've made are lost.

4 **View presentation with new design:**

On **View** menu, choose **Slide Show** (or click 🖥️).

Click mouse button to advance from slide to slide.

If you do not like new design, you can follow above procedure to apply another one. New design replaces previous one.

5 **Save presentation with design as new file:**

On **File** menu, choose **Save As**.

Save with name **Slides with Design** on floppy disk.

Name indicates presentation has design template applied.

Tip
It's usually a good idea to keep a copy of a presentation without a design. That makes it easier to go back and make changes.

6 **Close presentation file:**

On **File** menu, choose **Close**.

Slides file as completed on page 88 must be on floppy disk.

Create speaker notes

Each slide has a speaker's notes page where you can write anything you want to be reminded of during the presentation.

1 **Open Slides file.**

2 **View speaker notes pages:**

Click ⬚ (notes page view button) at lower left of window.

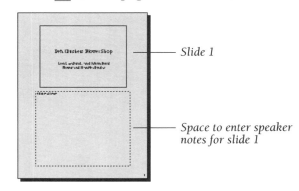

— *Slide 1*

— *Space to enter speaker notes for slide 1*

Use PAGE UP and PAGE DOWN to browse through slides and speaker notes.

Notice that there is one speaker note area for each slide.

By the way
You would not use speaker notes on the screen, of course. You print them and use the printed copy during your presentation. See page 112 for the details of printing.

3 **View notes master:**

On **View** menu, choose **Master**; on submenu, choose **Notes Master**.

Tip
The notes master works just like the slide master. Additions and changes here affect all notes pages.

4 **Select text block and enlarge font:**

Carefully click border of lower text block on notes master.

Whole text box is selected now.

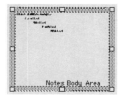

On font size list on formatting toolbar, choose **18**.

By the way
You can also press and drag to highlight individual blocks of characters, and use different sizes, fonts, and styles on the selection.

5 *Add header to notes pages:*

Click **Header Area** text box (at upper left).

Type **Petal Pushers Flower Shop** and tap ENTER.

6 *Add date to notes pages:*

On **View** menu, choose **Header and Footer**.

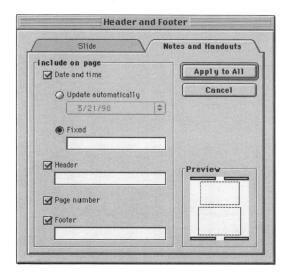

Click **Update automatically**, then choose format you like from pop-up list.

Click **Apply to All**.

7 *View individual notes pages:*

Click 🖳 (notes page view button). Use PAGE DOWN to see all pages.

Changes you made on master affected all notes pages.

Tap ⌘ HOME to move to notes page 1.

8 *Enter speaker notes for page 1:*

Click text placeholder in notes area.

Type following text. Tap RETURN between sentences.

> **This first slide should be displayed as the audience enters.**
>
> **Take a deep breath and count to 10 before proceeding.**

9 *Rename, save, and close presentation file:*

On **File** menu, choose **Save As**.

Save file with name **Notes**.

On **File** menu, choose **Close**.

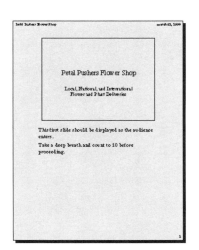

STOP *Slides file as completed on page 88 must be on floppy disk.*

Create audience handouts

To assist note takers, you can create audience handouts with two, three, or six slide miniatures on a page.

By the way
The handout master has separate layouts for each possible format of slide miniatures you can use. You choose the format you want when printing.

1 **Open Slides file.**

2 **View handout master:**

On **View** menu, choose **Master**; on submenu, choose **Handout Master**.

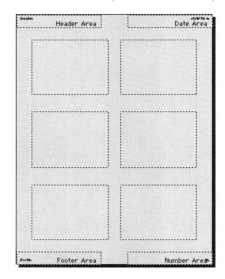

Changes you make on handout master affect all handout pages when they're printed. (You can't preview individual handout pages on screen.)

3 **View different handout formats available:**

Click buttons on **Handout Master** palette to see different formats.

4 **Add title to handout pages:**

Click **Header Area** text box.

Type **Petal Pushers Flower Shop**.

Click outside text box to end editing.

5 **Add date to handouts pages:**

See steps on page 109.

6 **Rename, save, and close presentation file:**

Click ▢ (slide view button) to return to slide view.

On **File** menu, choose **Save As**.

Save file with name **Handouts**.

On **File** menu, choose **Close**.

On page 112, you'll learn how to print your audience handouts.

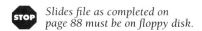 *Slides file as completed on page 88 must be on floppy disk.*

Print as overhead slides

With transparency film in your printer, you can print overhead slides directly from your presentation file.

1 **Open Slides file.**

2 **View Print dialog box:**

On **File** menu, choose **Print**. Note all **General** options available.

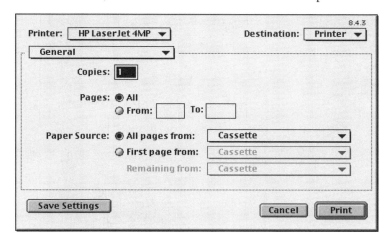

3 **Choose how many copies and which slides to print:**

In **Copies** text box, type number. In **Pages** area, select **All** or enter range.

4 **Choose PowerPoint options:**

On pop-up list below **Printer** label, choose **Microsoft PowerPoint**.

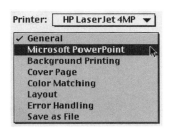

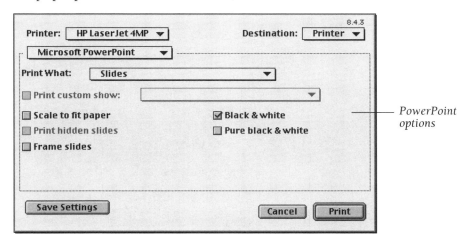

PowerPoint options

5 **Print slides.**

If you're printing overheads, make sure transparency film is loaded in paper tray you're using.

Click **Print** to start printing.

6 **Close file without saving changes when finished.**

Notes (page 108) and Handouts (page 110) files must be on floppy disk.

Print notes & handouts

You can also print the speaker notes and audience handouts you created earlier.

1 **Open Notes file.**

2 **Prepare to print:**

On **File** menu, choose **Print**.

In **Copies** text box, type number.

In **Pages** area, enter a range.

By the way

The figure and steps here are for computers using Mac OS 8. If you are using System 7.6 or earlier, the steps will be slightly different.

3 **Choose what to print.**

On pop-up list below **Printer** label, choose **Microsoft PowerPoint**.

Click or press down arrow to show **Print What** pop-up menu.

You can print only one thing at a time.

Choose **Notes Pages**.

Click **Print** to start printing.

Close file without saving changes when finished.

4 **Open Handouts file.**

5 **Prepare to print:**

On **File** menu, choose **Print**.

In **Copies** text box, type number.

In **Pages** area, enter a range.

6 **Choose what to print.**

On pop-up list below **Printer** label, choose **Microsoft PowerPoint**.

Click or press down arrow to show **Print What** pop-up menu.

Choose **Handouts** layout you want.

Click **Print** to start printing.

Close file without saving changes when finished.

7 **Quit Microsoft PowerPoint.**

This completes your work with Microsoft Powerpoint.

Start Microsoft Excel

You are now ready to start the Microsoft Excel application running on your computer.

1 *Start computer and Excel:*

Switch on computer (see page 2).

Start Microsoft Excel (see page 7, but choose **Microsoft Excel** this time).

If **Office Assistant** appears, click **Start using Microsoft Excel**. Then close **Office Assistant** window.

2 *View document window for Microsoft Excel:*

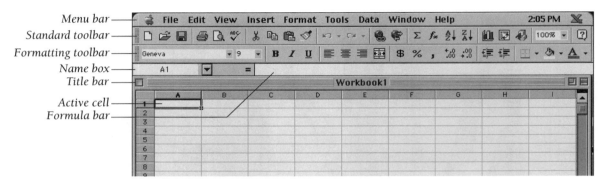

Menu bar

Standard toolbar

Formatting toolbar

Name box

Title bar

Active cell

Formula bar

Place pointer on any icon on either toolbar. *Do not click!*

Name of tool appears below pointer.

3 *Notice thick border around cell A1.*

Border indicates active cell. This is where data will appear when you type.

4 *Explore workbook:*

Look at tabs near bottom of window.

Microsoft Excel files are called workbooks. Each new workbook normally contains three blank worksheets, ready for use.

To switch to different sheet, click its tab once.

If you double-click by accident, press ⌈ESC⌉ key on keyboard. Active worksheet tab is white; others are gray.

Note four buttons to left of sheet tabs.

Buttons are for scrolling to any sheet tabs not visible. Currently you see all.

Click **Sheet1** to make worksheet 1 active.

Complete previous activity
before going on.

Select cells

*A worksheet consists of columns and rows. The intersection of
a column and a row forms a rectangle called a cell.*

1 **Select one cell:**

Move pointer over worksheet. Note shape:

Click pointer in any cell.

> *Active cell border moves to cell you selected.*

Click in cell A1.

2 **Note active cell name in name box at left of formula bar:**

> *Name is column letter plus row number of active cell on worksheet.*

Click another cell.

> *Notice that cell name changes in formula bar.*

By the way

Note that the column letter and row
number headings of the active cell
are emphasized.

3 **Practice keyboard moves:**

Tap [RETURN] to move *down* one cell.

Tap [SHIFT][RETURN] to move *up* one cell.

Tap [TAB] to move *right* one cell.

Tap [SHIFT][TAB] to move *left* one cell.

Tap →, ←, ↑, ↓ to move one cell in direction of arrow.

4 **Select range of cells (method 1):**

With pointer inside cell A1, press mouse button and drag pointer to cell C3.

> *Rectangular range (multiple cells) is selected (highlighted). Note that first
> cell remains white. This is active cell in range.*

5 **Deselect range:**

Click any cell on worksheet.

6 **Select range of cells (method 2):**

Click cell at upper left of range, hold down [SHIFT], and click lower-right cell.

7 **Select range of cells (method 3):**

Click cell at one corner of range.

With [SHIFT] held down, tap arrow keys to "paint" (or "unpaint")
highlighting in direction of arrow.

❗ *A new worksheet must be open.*

Enter text

Entering data is usually the first step in creating a spreadsheet. Text is entered by selecting a cell, then typing.

1 *Enter text in cell A1:*

Click cell A1.

Watch formula bar as you type **Petal Pushers Flower Shop**.

> *Use* DELETE *to erase typing errors.*

Note ☒ (cancel) and ☑ (enter) buttons now on formula bar:

2 *Accept entry in cell:*

Click ☑ on formula bar, or tap RETURN or TAB or arrow keys on keyboard.

> *Active cell stays A1 if you click* ☑*, changes if you use keyboard. Notice that cancel and enter buttons are gone. They appear only during data entry.*

3 *Select new cell and enter text:*

Click cell A3 and type **Rose**.

Tap RETURN on keyboard.

> *Data is entered. Active cell becomes A4.*

4 *Enter more data and accept it:*

Type **Pansy**.

Tap RETURN to enter data and move down to next cell.

> *Active cell should now be A5.*

5 *Enter data, then change mind:*

Type **Tulip**.

Click ☒ on formula bar, or tap ESC on keyboard.

> *Cell is unchanged.*

6 *Enter data again, then accept it:*

Type **Twolip** (yes, it's misspelled).

Tap RETURN to enter data and move down.

> *Active cell should now be A6.*

Type **Daisy**.

Click ☑ on formula bar to end data entry and leave cell active.

> **Tip**
> *Remember that your entry is not complete until you click the enter button (or use another technique to end editing). If some Excel commands don't seem to be working, look at the formula bar. If you see the cancel and enter buttons there, it means you forgot to complete your entry.*

> **Tip**
> *If you have a Macintosh with an extended keyboard, including a numeric keypad on the right side, you can use the* ENTER *key to end editing and remain in cell. The* RETURN *key and* ENTER *key function differently. The* ENTER *key functions like the enter button on the formula bar.*

7 *Correct errors, delete characters (method 1):*

Click cell with error to be corrected (A5).

In formula bar, click I-beam pointer just right of error (**wo**).

Insertion point appears where you clicked.

Tap DELETE twice to erase error characters, then type **u**.

Tap RETURN or click ✓ on formula bar to accept editing.

8 *Replace data already in cell:*

Click cell A6 if necessary.

Once cell is selected, just type new information.

Type **Daffodill** and tap RETURN to accept change.

Daffodill replaces Daisy in cell A6.

9 *Correct errors, delete characters (method 2):*

Daffodil is spelled incorrectly.

Double-click cell A6 in worksheet.

This time, insertion point appears in cell, not formula bar.

Position I-beam pointer just right of either **l**.

Tap DELETE to erase error.

Tap RETURN or click ✓ on formula bar to accept change.

10 *Delete data in cell:*

Click cell A1.

On **Edit** menu, choose **Clear**; on submenu, choose **All**.

You can also use DEL for this. Key is left of END.

11 *Undo and redo previous change:*

On **Edit** menu, choose **Undo Clear** or tap ⌘ Z.

On **Edit** menu, choose **Redo Clear** or tap ⌘ Y.

Text is cleared again.

Click ↶▾ (undo button) on standard toolbar.

Text is entered again.

By the way

Note that the Undo *command now shows the next step you can undo.* You can undo multiple actions using *the list on the undo tool on the standard toolbar.*

Save workbook file

After creating and editing a new workbook file, you should save it permanently on disk.

1 *Insert floppy disk:*

Insert disk, slider end first with label side up, into floppy drive.

2 *Give Save command:*

On **File** menu, choose **Save** (or click 🖫 on standard toolbar).

3 *Name workbook file:*

Note current file name (Workbook1) is highlighted in **Save as** text box.

Type **Sales** in text box.

Use DELETE to erase errors.

Typing replaces highlighted text.

4 *Say where to save document:*

Click ⬜ **Desktop** (desktop button) at right of dialog box.

Double-click 🖫 **Work Disk** (floppy disk icon) on list in center of dialog box.

Save dialog box should look like figure below.

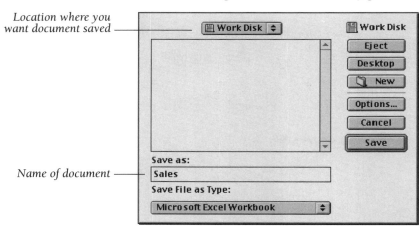

Location where you want document saved

Name of document

Click **Save** to save document with name **Sales** on floppy disk.

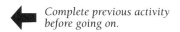 *Complete previous activity before going on.*

Enter numbers & save

As you'll soon see, the power of spreadsheets lies in their ability to do calculations with numerical data.

1 *Enter numbers in column B:*

> *Column B will contain the quantity (in dozens) of each flower sold in month.*

Click cell B3.

Type **1 9** .

Tap RETURN .

> *Active cell is now B4.*

Type **2 9** and tap RETURN .

> *Active cell is now B5.*

Type **2 2** and tap RETURN .

> *Active cell is now B6.*

Type **8** and tap RETURN .

Tip

You can enter numbers using the keys at the top of the standard keyboard or on the numeric keypad on the right side of the keyboard.

2 *Add sales data for next month in column C:*

Click cell C3.

Type **1 8** and tap RETURN .

> *Active cell is now C4.*

Type **3 4** and tap RETURN .

> *Active cell is now C5.*

Type **2 5** and tap RETURN .

> *Active cell is now C6.*

Type **1 0** and tap RETURN .

3 *Enter numbers for next month in column D:*

Finish entering data to duplicate this spreadsheet:

	A	B	C	D
1	Petal Pushers Flower Shop			
2				
3	Rose	19	18	15
4	Pansy	29	34	36
5	Tulip	22	25	35
6	Daffodil	8	10	14
7				

4 *Save changed document:*

On **File** menu, choose **Save** (or click 🖫 on standard toolbar).

> *No dialog box appears this time. Changed workbook file replaces previously saved version on floppy disk. Original is permanently erased!*

Highlight cells

Many commands affect only the cells that you highlight (select) before giving the command.

1 *Highlight whole spreadsheet:*

Click empty box above row 1 and to left of column A.

All cells are highlighted. Different highlighting (white) shows A1 is active.

2 *Highlight one whole column:*

Click  (header for column A).

First cell in column is active cell.

3 *Highlight several whole columns:*

With pointer inside column B header, press mouse button and drag to right to highlight columns C and D.

Note text box indicating number of columns. Release mouse button.

4 *Highlight one row, then several rows:*

Click ![3 Rose] (header for row 3).

Whole row is highlighted.

Press inside row 3 header (*not* line between row headers) and drag down to highlight rows 4, 5, and 6. Note which cell is active.

5 *Highlight separated rows:*

Click header for row 1.

Hold down ⌘ and click headers for rows 4 and 6. Note active cell.

⌘ lets you add any cells you want to current selection.

Click any cell to deselect block.

6 *Highlight data area:*

Click cell A3.

Hold SHIFT down and click cell D6.

Active cell is A3.

7 *Move through selected cells:*

Observe active cell as you tap TAB repeatedly.

Try same with RETURN and ENTER.

This is convenient way to enter large amounts of data in table.

8 *Close workbook without saving changes:*

On **File** menu, choose **Close**.

If asked whether to save changes, click **Don't Save**.

Enter simple formulas

You can enter simple formulas in spreadsheets using keyboard or mouse.

1 *Open new workbook file:*

Click ◻ (new tool) on standard toolbar.

2 *Enter numbers to create following worksheet:*

	A	B	C	D
1				
2				
3	123	321	741	1417
4	456	654	852	2582
5	789	987	963	3693

3 *Save workbook:*

On **File** menu, choose **Save**.

Save on floppy disk with name **Number Practice**.

4 *Enter formula (method 1):*

Click cell A7.

> *Row 6 is "insurance" row for later additions between data and formulas.*

Type **=**.

> *Formulas always begin with =.*

Type **a3+a4**.

> *You don't have to type capital letters for cell names.*

Tap (ENTER) or click ✓ (enter button) on formula bar to compl]

5 *Observe formula and results:*

Look at formula bar and worksheet cell A7.

> *Cell A7 has two things in it. You see formula you ente formula bar. You see result (579) on worksheet.*

Click outside cell A7.

> *Result stays on worksheet, but formula is not i*

Click cell A7 to see formula again.

6 *Enter formula (method 2):*

Click cell B7 and type **=**.

Click cell B3 (or use arrow keys to m

Type **+**.

Click cell B4 (or use arrow keys

Tap (ENTER) or click ✓ to acc'

Tip

If you see a number in a cell, how can you tell whether the entry in the cell is the number itself or a formula that results in the number? Simple: Just click the cell and look at the formula bar. The formula bar always shows what was entered in the cell.

Enter simple formulas *continued*

7   *Observe results.*

Formula bar should contain =B3+B4. Cell B7 should show 975.

8   *Enter subtraction formula:*

Click cell B8 and type **=** .

Tap ⬆ or click to select cell B7.

Type **-** .

Tap ⬆ and ⬅ or click to select cell A7.

Tap ENTER or click ✓. Check formula and result.

Formula should read =B7–A7. Result in cell B8 should be 396.

9   *Enter multiplication formula:*

Click cell B10.

Use any method to enter formula **=B7 * B8** .

For asterisk (*) tap SHIFT 8 *or use key on numeric keypad.*

Tap ENTER or click ✓. Check formula and result.

Result in cell B10 should be 386100.

10 *Enter division formula:*

Click cell B12.

Use any method to enter formula **=B7 / A7** .

Slash (/) is on both main keyboard and numeric keypad.

Tap ENTER or click ✓. Check formula and result.

Result in cell B12 should be 1.683938.

11 *Enter more complex formula:*

Click cell B14.

Use any method to enter formula **=A3+A4+B3+B4** .

Tap ENTER or click ✓. Check formula and result.

Result in cell B14 should be 1554.

12 *Close workbook WITHOUT saving changes:*

On **File** menu, choose **Close**.

Click **Don't Save** in message box when asked whether to save changes.

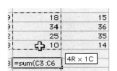

Use function to add

Microsoft Excel has many functions you can use in formulas for such tasks as adding up a column or a row of numbers.

1 **Open Sales:**

On **File** menu (in bottom section), choose **Sales**.

Microsoft Excel lists last four files you opened at bottom of File *menu.*

2 **Enter formula with function (method 1):**

Click cell B8, where result of formula will appear.

Type **=sum(b3:b6)**.

Colon (:) is on key to right of ⌊L⌋. *Formula uses SUM function to add numbers in cell range B3:B6. (You don't have to use capital letters when typing function names or cell names.)*

Tap ⌈ENTER⌉ or click ✓. Check formula and result.

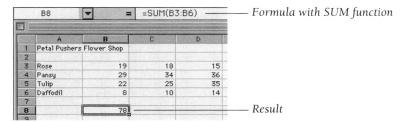

— *Formula with SUM function*

— *Result*

3 **Enter formula with function (method 2):**

Click cell C8, where result of second formula will appear.

Type **=sum(**.

Put pointer in cell C3. Press and drag down to cell C6. Release mouse button.

When you're entering formulas, dragging through cells enters cell range.

Tap ⌈ENTER⌉ or click ✓. Note that Excel enters closing parenthesis for you.

Check formula and result.

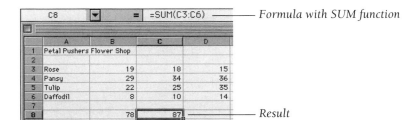

— *Formula with SUM function*

— *Result*

4 **Delete both formulas:**

Highlight cells B8 and C8.

On **Edit** menu, choose **Clear**, then **All** (or tap ⌈DEL⌉).

5 **Enter formula with function (method 3, works only for SUM function):**

Click cell B8, where result of formula will appear.

On standard toolbar, click Σ (AutoSum tool).

> *Formula =SUM(B3:B7) appears in formula bar (and on worksheet) with cell range highlighted. Entry isn't complete yet.*

Tap (ENTER) or click ✓. Check result.

> *Results are same as in step 2.*

> **By the way**
> *The extra cell in the range (B6) does not contain a number and so will not affect the result. The SUM function ignores blank cells and cells containing text.*

6 **Use AutoSum again:**

Click cell C8, where result will appear.

On standard toolbar, click Σ again.

Check formula.

> *Formula =SUM(C3:C7) should appear.*

Tap (ENTER) or click ✓. Check result.

> *Results are same as in step 3.*

7 **Use AutoSum once more:**

Click cell D8, where result will appear.

On standard toolbar, click Σ again.

Check formula.

> *Oops! Formula this time is not correct: =SUM(B8:C8). AutoSum picks closest data range and in this case is wrong. Cell range is already highlighted in formula, so it's easy to change.*

On worksheet, press and drag from cell D3 down to cell D7.

> *Note that formula in formula bar (and on worksheet) changes. Formula should be =SUM(D3:D7). If not, delete range then press and drag again.*

Tap (ENTER) or click ✓. Check result.

> *Correct sum is 100.*

> **By the way**
> *You can also edit the formula by typing in corrected ranges.*

8 **Enter label for sums:**

Click cell A8. Type **Total** and tap (RETURN).

9 **Save workbook file:**

On **File** menu, choose **Save**.

> *Edited version of Sales replaces previous version on floppy disk.*

Copy formula (relative)

Microsoft Excel's AutoFill feature allows you to copy formulas from one cell to many other cells quickly and easily.

1 *Enter title for totals in column E:*

Click cell E2. Type **Totals by Flower** and tap RETURN.

2 *Enter another addition formula using AutoSum:*

With cell E3 active, click Σ (AutoSum tool) on standard toolbar.

Verify formula.

> *Formula should be =SUM(B3:D3), since B3:D3 is closest range of numbers.*

Tap ENTER or click ✓ to accept formula.

Check result on worksheet; should be **52**.

3 *Copy formula to other cells (method 1, using AutoFill):*

Position pointer over small square in lower-right corner of active cell border.

> *Small square is AutoFill handle. Note that pointer changes shape.*

Press and drag down to cell E6.

> *Notice outline that surrounds range where data is to copy.*

Release mouse button.

> *Formula is copied down. You can also use AutoFill to copy up, copy left, and copy right. Direction depends on where you drag AutoFill handle.*

Click any cell containing copied formula. Look at formula bar.

> *Cell names have changed from original (B3:D3) to be "relative" to location of copy of formula. For example, if copy is in row 4, range is B4:D4.*

> **Tip**
> The pointer must be in a precise location for AutoFill to work. Watch for the proper pointer shape.

4 *Copy formula (method 2, using Copy and Paste):*

Click cell D8. Note formula in formula bar.

On **Edit** menu, choose **Copy**.

Click cell E8.

On **Edit** menu, choose **Paste** (or simply tap ENTER; *do not use* RETURN).

Verify result is **265** and that cell names have changed in copy so it sums numbers in column E.

> **By the way**
> You MUST use method 2 when the cell where you want the copy is not next to the cell with the original.

5 *Save changed workbook file:*

On **File** menu, choose **Save**.

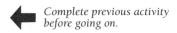

Create data series

*The AutoFill feature also helps enter standard data in a series,
such as months, years, or quarters.*

> **By the way**
> *AutoFill also works with days of the
> week. If you begin the series with an
> abbreviation, such as Jan or Wed,
> or if you use all capital letters, the
> rest of the series follow your example.*

1 **Enter first item in series:**

Click cell B2.

Type **January** and tap (ENTER) or click ☑.

2 **Create series of months:**

Press AutoFill handle carefully and drag to surround range B2 through D2.

Note text box indicator.

Release mouse button.

> *Cell C2 now contains* February *and D2 contains* March.

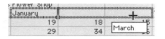

3 **Save changed workbook file.**

4 **Try another data series:**

Click cell B2. Type **1998** and tap (ENTER) or click ☑.

Press and drag AutoFill handle to surround range B2 through D2.

Release mouse button.

Look at cells C2 and D2.

> *Both contain 1998. AutoFill tool simply copies numbers.*

5 **Use Fill Series command to create series of years:**

Cells B2 through D2 should still be selected.

On **Edit** menu, choose **Fill**; then, on submenu, choose **Series**.

> *Type of series is* Linear *and Step Value is 1. That's what you want now.*

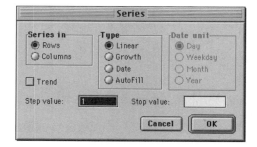

Click **OK** or tap (ENTER).

> *Cell C2 now contains 1999 and D2 contains 2000.*

6 **Close workbook file without saving changes:**

On **File** menu, choose **Close**.

Click **Don't Save** in message box asking whether to save changes.

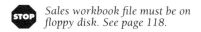
Copy formula (absolute)

Relative change of cell names is normally what you want in a copy of a formula—but not always. Here's an example.

1 *Open Sales.*

2 *Create new column title:*

Click cell F2. Type **Percent of Total** and tap `RETURN` to move down.

> **By the way**
> When text is entered in cell F2, text in E2 appears truncated. It is still there, but no longer displayed. You will fix this later.

3 *Calculate percentages:*

> *Column F will show each flower's total sales as percentage of grand total (265 in cell E8).*

With cell F3 active, use any method to enter formula **=E3/E8**.

> *Result is 0.196226. You want this shown as a percentage.*

With cell F3 active, click (percent style tool) on formatting toolbar.

> *Same number now appears as 20%.*

4 *Copy formula down column:*

Press and drag AutoFill handle down to cell F6. Release mouse button.

> *Oops! Something is wrong! Error message #DIV/0 means formula is trying to divide number by zero.*

5 *View formulas in cells on worksheet:*

On **Tools** menu, choose **Preferences**. If necessary, click **View** tab.

In **Window options** area, click to put mark in **Formulas** check box.

Click **OK**.

Scroll so columns E and F are both in view.

	C	D	E	F
1				
2	February	March	Totals by Flower	Percent of Total
3	18	15	=SUM(B3:D3)	=E3/E8
4	34	36	=SUM(B4:D4)	=E4/E9
5	25	35	=SUM(B5:D5)	=E5/E10
6	10	14	=SUM(B6:D6)	=E6/E11
7				

Look at formula in cell F4.

> *Formula is =E4/E9. There is no number in cell E9.*

Look at formulas in cells F5 and F6.

> *You wanted E3 to change relative to new location, but E8 needs to remain constant in each copy of original formula.*

6 *Make divisor stay same in copies:*

Double-click cell F3.

Put insertion point between **E** and **8**.

Type **$**   (SHIFT 4) and tap ENTER or click ✓ .

> *Formula should be =E3/E$8. Dollar sign makes 8 absolute. It won't change in copies. The 3 in E3 is still relative. It will change in copies in other rows.*

Press and drag AutoFill handle again to surround range F3:F6.

Release mouse button and look at copies this time.

> *The 8 in E8 remains constant ("absolute") in all copies of formula.*

By the way

Cell names in formulas are often called "references" because they refer to the data in the cell. A dollar sign before a row letter or a column number makes it an "absolute reference."

	C	D	E	F
1				
2	February	March	Totals by Flower	Percent of Total
3	18	15	=SUM(B3:D3)	=E3/E$8
4	34	36	=SUM(B4:D4)	=E4/E$8
5	25	35	=SUM(B5:D5)	=E5/E$8
6	10	14	=SUM(B6:D6)	=E6/E$8
7				
8	=SUM(C3:C7)	=SUM(D3:D7)	=SUM(E3:E7)	

7 *View results in worksheet cells:*

On **Tools** menu, choose **Preferences**.

In **Window options** area, click to remove mark in **Formulas** check box.

Click **OK**.

Scroll so that column A is in view.

	A	B	C	D	E	F
1	Petal Pushers Flower Shop					
2		January	February	March	Totals by Flo	Percent of Total
3	Rose	19	18	15	52	20%
4	Pansy	29	34	36	99	37%
5	Tulip	22	25	35	82	31%
6	Daffodil	8	10	14	32	12%
7						
8		78	87	100	265	

> *Percentages appear correctly with new formulas.*

8 *Save changed workbook:*

On **File** menu, choose **Save**.

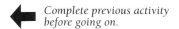

Paste function

The AVERAGE function averages numbers in a range on a worksheet. It is easily inserted using Paste Function dialog box.

1 ***Add another text label to worksheet:***

Click cell A9.

Type **Average** and tap ⌜RETURN⌝.

2 ***Enter formula in cell to right of label:***

Click cell B9 and type **=** to begin formula.

This is cell where average sales for January will appear.

On **Insert** menu, choose **Function**.

Paste Function *dialog box appears.*

In **Function category** list, choose **Most Recently Used**.

In **Function name** list, choose **AVERAGE**.

AVERAGE *is also listed under* Statistical *category.*

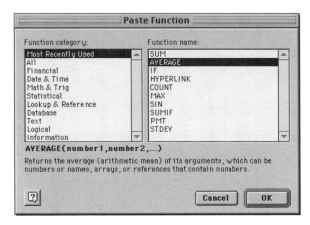

Click **OK** button.

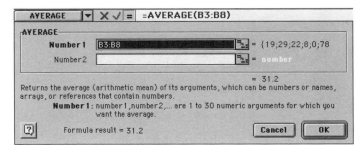

Click (collapse dialog button) to reduce size of dialog box so you can see worksheet data.

On worksheet, drag to highlight range B3:B6 (January cells to be averaged).

Click (expand dialog button) to restore size of dialog box.

Click **OK**.

Formula is inserted and result, 19.5, appears on worksheet.

3 *Copy formula to other months and total:*

Press carefully and drag AutoFill handle to surround range B9:E9.

Release mouse button.

Verify that results are **21.75, 25,** and **66.25** and that cell addresses have changed to be relative to new locations of copies.

4 *Add another label to worksheet:*

Click cell A10.

Type **Maximum** and tap (RETURN).

5 *Add MAX function:*

Click cell B10 and type **=** to begin formula.

On **Insert** menu, choose **Function**.

In **Function category** list, choose **Most Recently Used**.

In **Function name** list, choose **MAX** (maximum).

Click **OK** button.

Click ▣ (collapse dialog button), then highlight range B3:B6 on worksheet.

Click ▣ (expand dialog button), then click **OK**.

Formula is inserted and result, 29, *appears on worksheet.*

Copy formula to range C10:E10.

Verify that results are **34, 36,** and **99** and that cell addresses have changed to be relative to new locations of copies.

6 *Add another function in next row:*

Type **Minimum** label in cell A11.

Click cell B11 and type **=** to begin formula.

On **Insert** menu, choose **Function**.

In **Function category** list, choose **All**.

In **Function name** list, choose **MIN** (minimum).

Follow steps above to add range B3:B6.

Copy formula to range C11:E11.

Verify that results are **8, 10, 14,** and **32** and that cell addresses have changed to be relative to new location.

7 *Save and close changed workbook file.*

Format text

After entering data, you may wish to format text to emphasize and clarify. You can use menu commands or toolbar buttons.

1 **Open Sales from your floppy disk.**

2 **Add bold style to labels (method 1, bold tool):**

Highlight range A1:F2 (title in row 1 and column labels in row 2).

> *Make sure pointer shape is big outlined plus sign, not small AutoFill pointer.*

On formatting toolbar, click **B** (bold tool).

> *Text in highlighted cells is bold. Note that bold tool is depressed.*

3 **Remove bold using bold tool:**

Click cell A1. Click **B** (depressed bold tool).

4 **Add bold labels (method 2, Format Cells command):**

Click column A header (above cell A1) to select whole column.

On **Format** menu, click **Cells**. Click **Font** tab in dialog box.

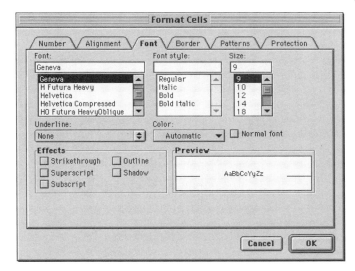

On **Font style** list, click **Bold**. Click **OK**.

5 **Add bold to other labels (method 3, format painter tool):**

Click any cell with bold text.

On standard toolbar, click (format painter tool).

Click header for row 8 (row of totals).

> *Format painter copies all formats from first cell (or block of cells) and "paints" them in whatever other cells you select.*

6 **Add italic to bold:**

Select cells A3 through A6. On formatting toolbar, click **I** (italic tool).

7 **Save changed workbook file.**

By the way

Not all text in a cell must be formatted the same way. To make some characters bold, for example, click the cell with the text, go to the formula bar, and highlight just those characters you want to be bold. Then apply bold format.

By the way

As you can see, the Format Cells dialog box lets you apply many different formats to the data in a cell. You'll use more of them soon.

Change fonts & font sizes

Text can appear in many different fonts and sizes. Each font specifies the shapes of all the letters, numbers, and symbols.

1 **Choose cell to apply format change to:**

Click cell A1.

> *Notice that text flows into cells B1 and C1 but is actually contained in cell A1. (Check formula bar.) Overflow is allowed when adjacent cell is empty.*

2 **Check current font and size:**

On formatting toolbar, note **Geneva** font in size **9**.

> *These are defaults on new worksheets.*

On formatting toolbar, click or press down arrow to view font list.

> *Your list of fonts may be different.*

3 **Change font and size:**

On font list, scroll down and choose **Times**.

> *Command affects only text in selected cell.*

On formatting toolbar, click or press down arrow to view font size list.

On font size list, choose **14**.

> *Notice that row height automatically adjusts to new font size.*

4 **Change font size of another range:**

Highlight cells in range A8:E8.

> *This is row of totals (if you did activity on page 123).*

On font size list, choose **10**.

5 **Save changed workbook file.**

Change text alignment

*Text can be aligned left, right, or center within a cell. It can also
be centered over a range.*

By the way

Notice that text labels normally
align to the left and numbers
normally align to the right. But you
can change that with the tools you
learn here.

1 *Align data within cells (method 1):*

Highlight range B2:F2 (column labels you began entering on page 126).

On formatting toolbar, locate four alignment tools.

Click ▤ (center tool).

Select range A8:A11 (function labels you entered on page 129).

On formatting toolbar, click ▤ (align right tool).

2 *Align data within cells (method 2):*

Highlight range B3:F11 (cells with numbers).

On **Format** menu, choose **Cells**.

Click **Alignment** tab.

Note standard alignment settings and many other options available.

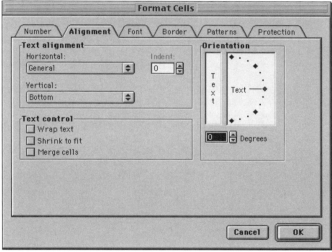

In **Horizontal** list, choose **Center**.

Click **OK**.

3 *Center title on selected columns:*

Select range A1:F1.

On formatting toolbar, click ▦ (center across columns tool).

Cells are merged into one large cell.

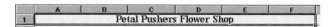

4 *Save changed workbook file.*

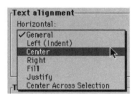

! *Sales workbook file must be open.*

Set column width & row height

You can easily change column widths and row heights, either one at a time or as a group.

1 *Change column width (method 1):*

Position pointer on right border of column E header.

When pointer changes shape, you can change width of column E.

You could drag left or right to change width. Here's a better way.

Double-click while pointer has above shape.

Width automatically adjusts to widest entry in column E.

Repeat above steps to adjust columns A and F.

2 *Change column width (method 2):*

Highlight any block of cells in columns B, C, and D.

On **Format** menu, choose **Column**; on submenu, choose **Width**.

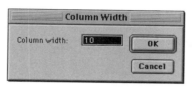

Type **8** and click **OK**.

Widths of all cells in all three columns are changed.

3 *Change row height (method 1):*

Carefully put pointer on bottom border of header for row 7 (blank row).

When pointer changes shape, you can change height of row above it.

Observe height in text box as you press mouse button.

Press and drag up to adjust height to **8** (points).

Height indicator in text box shows change as you make it.

If you drag too far, drag back down again.

4 *Change row height (method 2):*

Highlight any block of cells in rows 2 through 6.

On **Format** menu, choose **Row**; on submenu, choose **Height**.

Type **15** and click **OK**.

5 *Save changed workbook file.*

By the way

Another way to make a long label fit in a column is to make its text "wrap" inside its cell. The width of the column stays the same, and the height of the row expands to allow room for the wrapped text. To wrap text, use the Format Cells dialog box (see the figure on page 133 and note the Wrap Text *check box in the middle).*

Sales workbook file must be open.

Insert & delete cells

You can insert blocks of new cells, including whole rows and columns. You can also delete existing cells.

Insert
Cells...	⌘I
Rows	
Columns	
Worksheet	

1 *Insert whole column of new cells:*

Click any cell (except merged cell in row 1) in column B.

> *Active column will move right to make room for new column.*

On **Insert** menu, choose **Columns**.

> *New column of empty cells is inserted.*

2 *Insert whole row:*

Click any cell in row 6.

> *Active row will move down to make room for new row.*

On **Insert** menu, choose **Rows**.

> *New row of empty cells is inserted.*

3 *Insert multiple rows:*

Press and drag through headers to highlight rows 2 and 3.

> *Excel will insert as many rows as you select.*

On **Insert** menu, choose **Rows**.

> *Two new rows of empty cells are inserted.*

Click cell A2. Type **format test** and tap ⌈ENTER⌉ or click ☑.

> *Text is bold and large. New cell A2 got its text formats from cell A1. Each inserted cell inherits format from cell above (or at left if column is inserted).*

4 *Delete all cells in row:*

Click in header to highlight row 2.

On **Edit** menu, choose **Delete**.

By the way

You can also highlight and delete any block of cells. After choosing Delete on the Edit menu, you're asked how to move existing cells into the empty space after the block is removed. Notice this difference between deleting a cell and deleting the data in a cell. If you delete only the data (by choosing Clear on the Edit menu), other cells don't shift.

5 *Insert rectangular block of new cells:*

Highlight cells in range B3:C5.

On **Insert** menu, choose **Cells**.

> *Dialog box asks how to shift existing cells to make room for new block.*

Click **Shift cells down**. Click **OK** to see effect.

6 *Close workbook file without saving changes.*

Sales workbook file must be on floppy disk. See page 118.

136 / Spreadsheets with Microsoft Excel

Hide gridlines & add borders

You can hide the gray gridlines and add custom borders to cells and ranges. The Borders palette is an easy way to add borders.

1 **Open Sales from your floppy disk.**

2 **Follow directions in this section and next to duplicate figure below.**

3 **Hide gridlines:**

On **Tools** menu, choose **Preferences**.

Click **View** tab.

Under **Window options**, click to remove mark from **Gridlines** check box.

Click **OK**.

> *Standard gridlines no longer appear. You can add your own borders.*

4 **View Border palette in front of worksheet:**

On formatting toolbar, click or press arrow on [borders tool icon] (borders tool).

Put pointer on bar at top of palette. With mouse button held down, drag down until you see empty rectangle following pointer away from toolbar. Release mouse button.

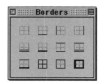

> *Each icon on palette shows where border line will be added to selected cells and what type of border (thin or thick) will appear.*

5 **Add outline border to whole data area:**

Highlight range A2:F11.

On **Border** palette, click thick-outline tool (lower-right corner).

Click any cell to deselect range and see thick borders around data area.

6 *Add bottom border (method 1):*

Highlight range A6:F6.

On **Border** palette, click thin bottom tool (first row, second column).

7 *Add bottom border (method 2):*

Highlight range B8:E8.

On **Format** menu, choose **Cells**; then click **Border** tab.

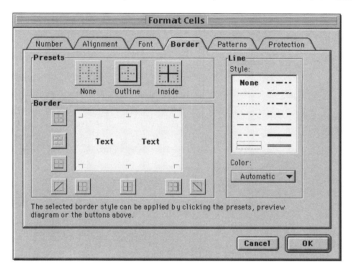

In **Style** area, click double line (last style in second column).

In **Border** area, click ⊞ (bottom border). Click **OK**.

8 *Add borders on right edges of cells:*

Highlight range A2:E11 (all but last column of table).

On **Format** menu, choose **Cells**; then click **Border** tab.

In **Style** area, click single medium line (last style in first column).

Click ⊞ and ⊞ to add borders between and to right sides of cells. Click **OK**.

9 *Remove and reapply borders:*

Highlight range A2:F11 (whole table).

On **Border** palette, click erase borders tool (first row and column).

On **Edit** menu, choose **Undo Borders** to restore borders.

10 *Close Border palette:*

At left of **Border** title bar, click ▣ (close box).

11 *Save changed workbook file.*

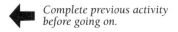
Add cell shading

You can also add a background color, a pattern, or a shade of gray to call attention to chosen cells.

1 **Add shading (method 1):**

Click or press down arrow on ⬛▾ (fill color tool). Put pointer on top bar and drag menu off as palette. Release mouse button.

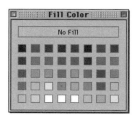

Color palette is torn off and remains in front of worksheet, ready for use.

Select cells in range B2:F2.

On **Color** palette, click to select any light color or shade of gray.

Click anywhere on worksheet to deselect cells.

When ready to close palette, click ▣ at left of **Fill Color** title bar.

2 **Add shading (method 2):**

Select range B8:E8.

On **Format** menu, choose **Cells**; then click **Patterns** tab.

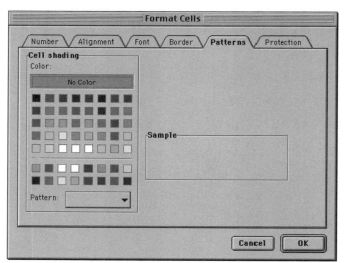

In **Color** area, click to select any light color or shade of gray.

Click arrow below colors to see **Pattern** list.

Choose any pattern with diagonal stripes.

Click **OK**.

Click anywhere on worksheet to deselect cells and see result.

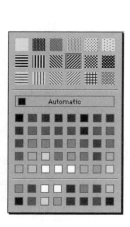

3 *Save and close Sales workbook file.*

Format numbers

Numbers on a worksheet can be formatted to appear with dollar signs, commas, and fixed decimal points.

1   Open Number Practice workbook file.

2   On formatting toolbar, observe number tools.

3   Apply number format (method 1):

Highlight range A3:D5.

On formatting toolbar, click $ (currency style tool).

> *Note that Microsoft Excel automatically increases column widths to accommodate new number format.*

4   Compare applied format with original data:

Click anywhere to deselect block.

$ 123.00	$ 321.00	$ 741.00	$ 1,417.00
$ 456.00	$ 654.00	$ 852.00	$ 2,582.00
$ 789.00	$ 987.00	$ 963.00	$ 3,693.00

> *Formatted numbers appear with dollar signs, comma separators, and two decimal places.*

Click any cell with number in new format. Look at formula bar.

> *Number remains as you entered it. Only format on worksheet has changed.*

5   Apply percent format:

Select same range of cells.

On formatting toolbar, click % (percent style tool). Deselect block.

6   Observe percent format.

12300%	32100%	74100%	141700%
45600%	65400%	85200%	258200%
78900%	98700%	96300%	369300%

> *Numbers appear with percent signs, no comma separators, no decimal places.*

7   Apply comma format:

Select same range of cells.

On formatting toolbar, click , (comma style tool).

> *Formatted numbers appear with comma separators, two decimal places, and no dollar signs.*

8 *Increase decimal places:*

If not highlighted, select data range A3:D5 again.

On formatting toolbar, click ⊞ (increase decimal tool).

Numbers appear with three decimal places.

Click ⊞ again to add another decimal place.

Microsoft Excel adjusts column widths to accommodate longer numbers.

9 *Decrease decimal places:*

On formatting toolbar, click ⊞ (decrease decimal tool) twice.

Numbers now have two decimal places.

Click ⊞ twice more.

Numbers appear with no decimal places.

10 *Change number format (method 2):*

If not highlighted, select data range A3:D5 again.

On **Format** menu, choose **Cells**, then click **Number** tab.

Current number format appears. Zero indicates fixed place; # indicates variable place; semicolon separates formats of positive and negative numbers.

Under **Category**, choose **General**.

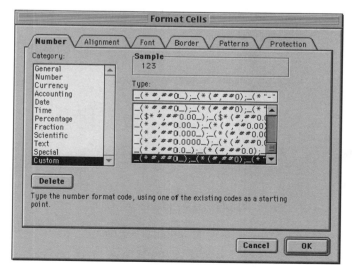

Click **OK**.

All special number formats are removed from selected cells.

11 *Close workbook file without saving changes.*

Enter & format dates

Dates can be formatted in many styles. They're treated as numbers so that you can perform calculations with them.

XLS / 141

1 **Open new workbook file:**

Click 🗋 (new tool) on standard toolbar.

2 **Enter date:**

Click cell B2.

Enter today's date in month/day/year format (example: 9/16/98).

Use two digits for year. Don't put leading zeros in month or day.

Tap (ENTER) or click ✓. Check formula bar.

Excel recognized entry as date and changed year to four-digit number.

Check worksheet cell.

Date appears on worksheet in format you used when entering data.

3 **View current date format and change it:**

On **Format** menu, choose **Cells**.

In Category list, Date is highlighted, showing that cell B2 contains date entry. Current format (m/d/yy) is highlighted in Type list.

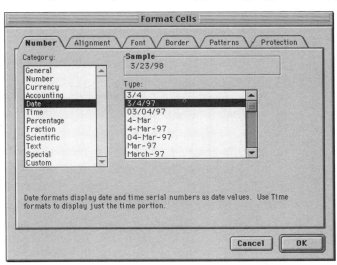

In **Type** list, click **4-Mar-97**. Click **OK**.

Format changes on worksheet, but entry (shown in formula bar) is same.

4 **Create new date format:**

On **Format** menu, choose **Cells**.

In **Category** list, click **Custom**.

Tap (TAB) until **Type** text box at top is highlighted.

Type **mmmm d, yyyy** and click OK.

Date appears in custom date format.

By the way

Years 1920–2019 may safely be entered in two-digit form. If you need to enter other years, you must type all four digits.

Perform date calculation

Dates really are numbers formatted in a special way so they appear as dates. You can do arithmetic with the numbers.

1 **Enter another date:**

Click cell B3. Type date of your next birthday in m/d/yy format.

Tap ⟨ENTER⟩ or click ☑ to accept entry.

2 **Apply new date format you created:**

With cell B3 selected, choose **Cells** on **Format** menu.

On **Category** list, click **Custom**. Scroll to bottom of **Type** list.

> *Your format (mmmm d, yyyy) is now listed.*

Click your new format. Click **OK**.

3 **Calculate how many days until your birthday:**

Click cell B5. Enter formula **=B3-B2**.

Tap ⟨ENTER⟩ or click ☑. Observe result.

> *Result equals number of days between two dates in calculation.*

4 **Change date formats to numbers and see what's happening:**

Highlight cells B2 and B3.

On **Format** menu, choose **Cells**. Look at **Category** list.

> *As expected, cells B2 and B3 have Date format. You'll now change it.*

On **Category** list, choose **General**.

Click **OK** and look at cells B2, B3, and B5.

> *All you changed was format. Dates really are numbers. That's why you can subtract one date from another and get a number. However, date numbers can appear in many different formats.*

5 **Find out what day 1 is:**

Click cell B7. Type **0** and tap ⟨ENTER⟩ or click ☑ to accept entry.

On **Format** menu, choose **Cells**.

Click **Number** tab if necessary.

On **Category** list, choose **Custom**.

On **Type** list, click your new date format. Click **OK**.

> *Day 0 is January 1, 1904. Dates are measured from then.*

6 **Close workbook file without saving changes:**

On **File** menu, choose **Close**.

Do not save changes.

By the way

Times work almost the same way as dates. You can subtract two times and get the time difference. However, the difference is formatted as a time, not a number. That way, you can read the difference directly in hours, minutes, and seconds.

Tip

If you're making changes in a worksheet, and if suddenly your dates disappear and strange five-digit numbers show up, it usually means your dates have lost their formats. Just highlight the numbers and reapply the date format you prefer. Your dates will reappear.

Sort data

You can rearrange the order of rows of cells in a spreadsheet. You can use the sort tool on the toolbar or the menus.

1 **Open Sales.**

2 **Select cells to be sorted:**

Highlight A3:D6 as in figure.

> *If you did not do all previous activities, formatting may be different.*

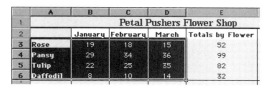

3 **Sort data so flower names are in alphabetical order (method 1):**

On standard toolbar, click ⬚ (sort ascending tool).

> *Rows are sorted alphabetically based on column with active cell (flower names). Notice that formulas in columns E and F still work properly.*

4 **Undo sort:**

On standard toolbar, click ↶▾ (undo tool) or tap ⌘ Z.

5 **Sort data so flower names are in alphabetical order (method 2):**

If same data is not still highlighted, select it again.

On **Data** menu, choose **Sort**.

> *Dialog box lets you choose column to sort on. You'll use column A.*

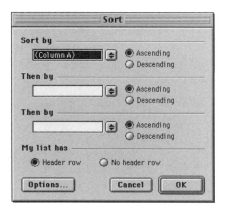

Click **OK**.

Deselect highlighted block.

6   *Use standard toolbar to sort data so top seller is first:*

Highlight A3:F6.

Tap TAB until cell E3 is active, as in figure.

2		January	February	March	Totals by Flower	Percent of Total
3	Daffodil	8	10	14	32	12%
4	Pansy	29	34	36	99	37%
5	Rose	19	18	15	52	20%
6	Tulip	22	25	35	82	31%

On standard toolbar, click ⬛ (sort descending tool).

Top seller (Pansy) is now in top row.

7   *Change sort to ascending by sales:*

On standard toolbar, click ⬛ (sort ascending tool).

Flower with lowest sales (Daffodil) is now in top row.

8   *Sort table with column labels in first row:*

Highlight range A2:F6.

Row 2 has column labels. You want only data to be sorted.

On **Data** menu, choose **Sort**.

If necessary, in **My list has** area at bottom of dialog box, click **Header row**.

Click arrow to see **Sort by** list.

Sort by list now has labels from top row of selected cells.

In **Sort by** list, choose **March**.

Click **Descending** radio button at top.

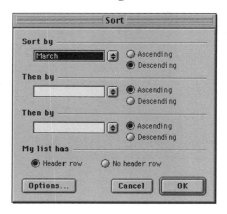

Click **OK**.

Data is now sorted in descending order of March sales.

9   *Close workbook without saving changes.*

Tip

Think of the Then by *areas of the* Sort *dialog box as "tie-breakers." If two rows of the selection have the same* Sort by *data, then the rows are sorted according to the data in the* Then by *columns.*

Divide window into panes

When a worksheet is large, it's handy to divide the window into panes that keep important parts in view.

1 Open Sales.

2 Split window into panes:

Split bar before window is divided

Press and drag split bar (above vertical scroll arrow) just below row 6.

— Split bar being dragged

Note that there are now two vertical scroll bars on right of window.

Use both scroll arrows in top pane to see whole worksheet.

Use both scroll arrows in bottom pane to see whole worksheet.

Each pane has separate view of same worksheet.

3 Lock labels in place in top pane:

In top pane, scroll so rows 1 and 2 (table and column labels) are at top.

Press and drag split bar just under row 2 in top pane.

On **Window** menu, choose **Freeze Panes**.

Split is now single line. Only one vertical scroll bar appears.

Use both scroll arrows to see what rows are available in lower pane.

Frozen rows in top pane

Scrolling rows in bottom pane

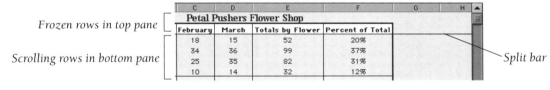

Split bar

Rows 1 and 2 are locked in top pane. Rest of worksheet scrolls in lower pane. Arrangement would be useful for table with many rows.

4 Unlock split:

On **Window** menu, choose **Unfreeze Panes**.

Split bar is double line. Two vertical scroll bars appear.

5 Remove window split:

Press and drag split bar to top of window.

You can also double-click split bar or give Remove Split *command on* Window *menu.*

6 Close workbook without saving any changes.

*Sales file must be on
floppy disk. See page 118.*

146 / *Spreadsheets with Microsoft Excel*

Lock cells & protect worksheet

*You can protect data in cells from accidental changes. Enter all
data and add all formatting before locking cells.*

1 **Open Sales.**

2 **Unlock cells where you want changes to be made:**

Highlight data cells in range B3:D6.

> *These cells will be unlocked for possible changes in sales numbers.*

On **Format** menu, choose **Cells**, then click **Protection** tab.

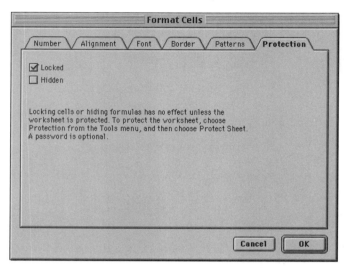

Click to remove mark from **Locked** check box, then click **OK**.

3 **Activate worksheet protection:**

On **Tools** menu, choose **Protection**, then **Protect Sheet**.

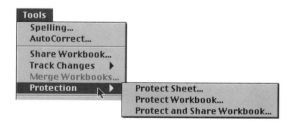

Click **OK**.

4 *Enter data in unlocked cell with protection turned on:*

Click cell B5. Type **100** and tap ENTER.

New data is entered and formulas recalculate.

5 *Try to enter data in locked cell with protection turned on:*

Click cell E5 and type **100**.

Locked cells message appears.

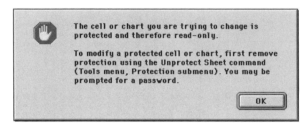

Click **OK**.

6 *Try to enter data in blank cell:*

Click cell G3 and type **100**.

Locked cells message appears again.

Click **OK**.

By the way

Protection is used mainly by people who design spreadsheets for other people to use. The designer wants the user simply to enter certain data but not to change formulas, labels, or even formats.

7 *Try to change format of any cell:*

Click cell B5 (unlocked). Try to click **B** (bold tool) to apply bold style.

Tool is grayed out telling you that no such change is allowed.

8 *Remove protection:*

On **Tools** menu, choose **Protection**, then **Unprotect Sheet**.

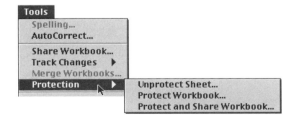

9 *Try to enter data in locked cell with protection turned off:*

Click cell E5, type **100** and tap ENTER.

Number is entered, replacing formula there.

10 *Close workbook without saving changes.*

STOP *Sales workbook file must be on floppy disk. See page 118.*

Make chart on worksheet

Once you create a worksheet table of numbers, you can quickly see a chart of the same data on the same worksheet.

1 Open Sales.

2 Select data to be charted:

Highlight range B2:D2 (names of months).

With ⌘ held down, highlight range B8:D8 (totals for months).

Both ranges should be highlighted.

3 Begin to create chart:

On **Insert** menu, choose **Chart**.

Step 1 of Chart Wizard *dialog box appears.*

If Office Assistant appears, click **No** to put it away.

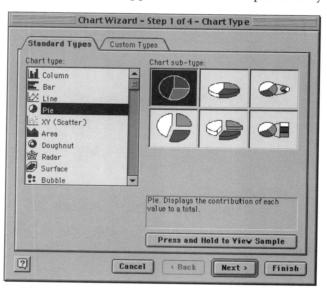

4 Choose chart type:

In **Chart type** list, click **Pie**.

In **Chart sub-type** accept default in upper left.

5 Click Next button to move to step 2.

Notice that Back *button becomes active. You can always go back through steps and make changes.* Cancel *closes the chart wizard without making the chart.* Finish *ends the charting process using default settings.*

6 *Verify data to be charted:*

Make sure **Data Range** text box contains **$B$2:$D$2,$B$8:$D$8**.

These are rows you highlighted in step 2. Dollar signs mean these cell references are absolute. They won't change if chart is moved.

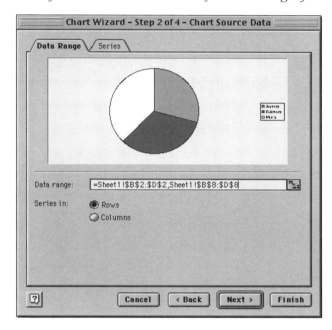

Click **Next** button to move to Step 3.

7 *Add chart options:*

Click tabs to review options.

You will make no changes here.

Tip

It is usually not necessary or desirable to add titles to a simple chart on the worksheet.

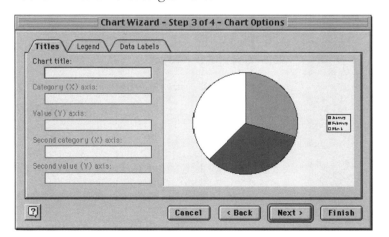

Click **Next** button to move to Step 4.

8   *Choose chart placement and see result:*

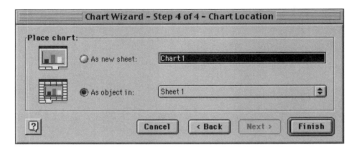

If necessary click **As object in**.

Click **Finish**.

Chart and chart toolbar appear on worksheet. Small black "handles" on edges of chart mean that chart is selected.

> **Tip**
>
> *If the chart toolbar is not present, click the chart area to select it. The toolbar appears only when the chart is selected.*
>
> *If it is still not available, choose* Chart *on the* View Toolbar *menu.*

Chart toolbar can be used to change chart type, add legend or gridlines.

9   *Adjust chart location:*

Place pointer inside chart area (but outside pie) and press and drag down below worksheet data.

10   *Change chart type:*

On chart toolbar, click or press down arrow to view Chart Type list.

Click ⬛ (3-D pie) as in figure at left.

Chart type changes to three-dimensional pie chart.

11   *See link between chart and worksheet data:*

Scroll up if necessary and click cell D6 (March daffodil sales).

You may have to move toolbar (by dragging title bar).

Type **1000** and tap [ENTER].

Scroll down if necessary to see changes in chart.

On standard toolbar, click 🔄 to undo editing change.

12   *Save changed workbook with new chart on worksheet.*

Make chart on separate sheet

You can also make a chart on a separate sheet in the workbook.
The chart and the data are still linked and will reflect changes.　　**XLS / 151**

1 *Select data to chart:*

Highlight range A2:D6 (monthly sales with row and column labels).

2 *Create chart on separate sheet:*

On **Insert** menu, choose **Chart**.

Step 1. Column should be selected as Chart type.

Click **3-D Column** as chart sub-type.

Click **Next**.

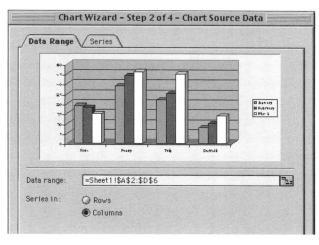

Step 2. Verify data to be charted is **$A$2:$D$6**. Click **Next**.

Step 3. Enter data for titles as in figure below.

Review other options.

　　You will make additional formatting changes later directly on chart.

Check preview. If necessary, go back to earlier steps and make changes.

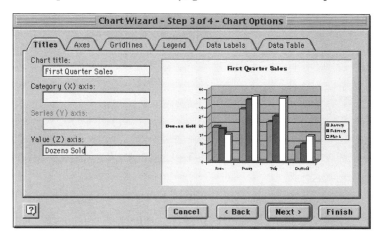

Click **Next**.

Step 4. Click **As new sheet**.

3 *View finished chart:*

Click **Finish**.

> *Chart is inserted as separate sheet (Chart1) in same workbook file. Chart toolbar is always present (unless you close it).*

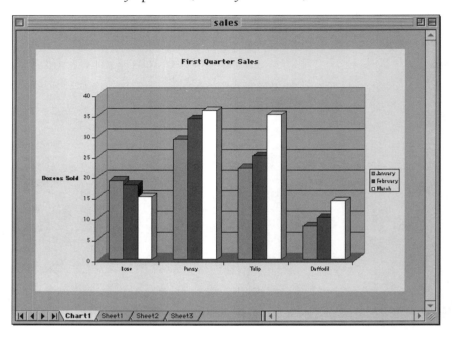

4 *Switch between sheet with chart and worksheet:*

At bottom of window, click **Sheet1** tab to see worksheet.

Click **Chart1** tab to return to sheet with chart.

5 *Go to worksheet and make change in data:*

Click **Sheet1** tab.

Click cell D3 (March sales of roses) and type **100**.

Tap (ENTER).

Click **Chart1** tab to see result in chart.

Compare with figure above.

Click 🔄 to undo change.

Click **Chart1** tab to see result of undo.

6 *Save changed workbook with new sheet.*

> *Worksheet and sheet with chart are saved together in same file.*

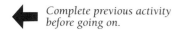
Format chart text

You can format any text on a chart. You can modify the font, font size, and/or font style.

1 *Format chart title:*

Click title on chart.

> *When selected, chart title has border with small black selection handles.*

On formatting toolbar, choose **Helvetica** on font list and **24** on font size list.

2 *Format legend:*

Click legend.

On formatting toolbar, choose **Helvetica** on font list and **12** on font size list.

On formatting toolbar, click **B** (bold tool) to add bold.

3 *Format and change orientation of value axis text label:*

Double-click axis label, **Dozens Sold**.

In dialog box, click **Font** tab.

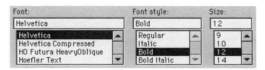

Choose **Helvetica** on font list and **12** on font size list.

Click **Alignment** tab.

In **Orientation** section, drag red diamond to top.

Verify that **Degrees** box contains **90**.

Click **OK**.

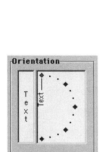

4 *Format value axis labels:*

Click value (vertical) axis.

Note text label and handles at ends.

On formatting toolbar, choose **Helvetica** on font list and **12** on font size list.

Click **B** (bold tool).

5 *Format category axis labels:*

Click category (horizontal) axis.

On formatting toolbar, choose **Helvetica** on font list and **12** on font size list.

Click **B** (bold tool).

6 *Save workbook:*

On **File** menu, choose **Save**.

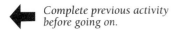

Complete previous activity before going on.

Format chart objects

You can format chart objects. You can change their color, their location, the axis scale, and other attributes.

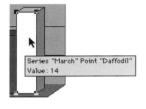

1 *Format data series:*

Click one column (data series) on chart.

> *When selected, data series has small black handles on each column.*

On **Format** menu, choose **Selected Data Series**. Click **Patterns** tab.

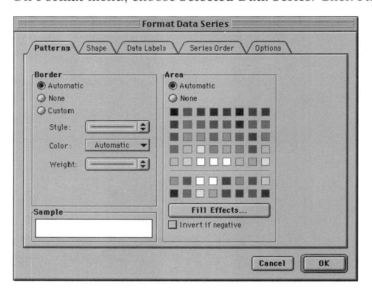

Using **Border** options, make any changes to borders of bars.

Using **Area** options, choose color and pattern for inside of bars.

Click **OK**.

> *Note*
>
> *Other tabs in this dialog box allow you to make changes to the series itself, its order and its values, and to add value, name, or percent labels to a data series.*

2 *Using steps above, make changes to other data series columns if you wish.*

3 *Change legend placement:*

Click legend.

On **Format** menu, choose **Selected Legend**.

Click **Placement** tab.

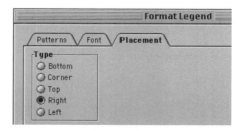

In **Type** area, click **Bottom**.

Click **OK**.

> *Legend moves to bottom of chart.*

4   *Change scale of vertical (value) axis:*

Click to select value axis:

On **Format** menu, choose **Selected Axis**.

Click **Patterns** tab.

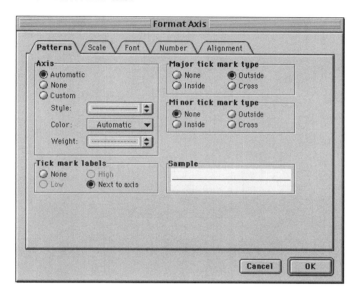

In **Major tick mark type**, click **Inside**.

Click **Scale** tab.

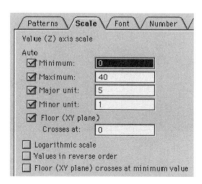

Change **Major unit** to 10.

Click **OK**.

5   *View chart with modifications.*

6   *Make additional changes to chart if you wish.*

7   *Save workbook with modified chart.*

Reorganize worksheets

*You can change the order in which sheets appear in a workbook,
and you can assign a name to a worksheet.*

1 *Move sheet tab:*

Point to **Chart1** tab at bottom of window.

Press and drag to move small triangle just right of **Sheet1** tab.

> *Notice small document icon that appears at end of pointer.*

Click **Sheet1** tab to activate worksheet.

> *It is now first sheet in workbook.*

2 *Name sheet:*

Double-click **Sheet1** tab.

> **By the way**
> You can use up to 31 characters for
> a sheet name.

Type **First Quarter Sales**.

> *New title replaces old.*

3 *Name chart:*

Use same method to name chart **First Quarter Sales Chart**.

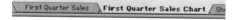

4 *Save workbook with changed sheet names and changed order of sheets.*

5 *Delete sheet with chart:*

Make sure **First Quarter Sales Chart** is active sheet.

On **Edit** menu, choose **Delete Sheet**.

> *Message means you can't undo deletion!*

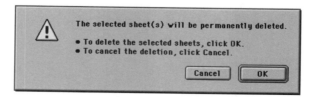

Click **OK**.

6 *Quit Microsoft Excel and end session at computer:*

On **File** menu, choose **Quit**.

Click **Don't Save** when asked whether to save changed file.

Shut down the Macintosh and switch off computer if necessary (see step 5, page 8).